Thought Poppers

Volume 1

Created By

Ronald J. Cohn

My old friend, Roy Devesh Carroll came up with the term "thought popper". He made me realize that as creator of this system, I'm not a philosopher like Immanuel Kant, David Hume, or Hannah Arendt; I'm more like the organ grinder man grinding out thought poppers for your enjoyment, elucidation, edification, enjoyment, pleasure and realization

---

To the Dadaist art of Marcel Duchamp
and to the wisdom of the sage Ashtavakra

Introduction

A phrase produced by a metaphorical monkey, a Philosophical Phrase Generator (PPG,) can be a thought popper when it works and a dud of poppycock when it doesn't. The flow coming from the Phrase Generator is composed of patterns of bits or splotches of ink which, if lit by a beam of consciousness, either has meaning or can be consigned to the categories of babble, balderdash, or gibberish.

This one could pop a few thoughts: "clashing unconsciousnesses"

The project began in early 1990's, after I read a great book, The Passion of the Western Mind by Richard Tarnas. It is a history of Western philosophy that reads like an exciting novel. When I finished reading the last page, I turned to the first one and started over again. I did the same thing with Ekhart Tolle's book The Power of Now. Also, I'm perennially involved with The Ashtavakra Gita, an ancient scripture in which the sage Ashtavakra instructs his disciple,
"You are that Consciousness, Supreme Bliss, upon which appears this phenomenal manifestation that is like the illusion of a snake on a rope. Know this and live happily."
The perception is illusory, like the fear that comes when you see a snake and then realize it's only a piece of rope. Contemporary *advaita* (Oneness) teacher, Rupert Spira, says that knowing the illusion of the snake upon the rope is only the first step, next comes knowing the rope. Oh, to always know the rope!

Now you know kind of where I'm coming from. Where I'm going is to know the rope.

When Richard Tarnas wrote in The Passion of the Western Mind that the "Journey to the East" was, in terms of Western intellectual history, just a branch of the Romantic Movement -- I fluttered my eye brows, twittered my nostrils, wiggled my ears, took some umbrage, and said to myself, "There's more to it than just the "RATIONAL WESTERN INTELLECTUAL TRADITION." I thought, Why, I could write a computer program that juggles up and overlays words like "Eastern", mystical", "gosh darned", and "super market" onto the phrase: "rational western intellectual tradition"... and so I did.
The PPG is a system of computer programs and a dictionary. The system can produce more than 24×10^{16} different phrases, that's over 24 *quadrillion* or 24,000 trillion phrases; a good number of which are nonsensical, but a surprising number of which are thought poppers that evoke some interesting meanings in an English knowing mind.

The PPG dictionary that I've assembled contains 9,240 adjectives or adjectival-phrases and 30,570 nouns or noun-phrases.. If they were each given an equal weighting, the generator would produce **purely random phrases.** But the dice that the monkey throws

down are loaded. Each word in the dictionary has a weighting factor that causes some words to appear more often than others. For example, "love" appears more often than "hate"; "beautiful" more often than "ugly"; and "health" more often than "sickness." The weightings are my personal choices. Certain words are omitted from the dictionary because they carry too much psychological weight. Such words dominate any phrase. These are words such as "concentration camp, "Nazi", and various words pertaining to body parts and specific bodily functions. One exception is the word "sex". It is in the dictionary and it will dominate any phrase in which it is the noun: e.g., "Republican sex," mathematical sex", or "rational Western intellectual sex." The rating for "sex" is such that it provides a light sprinkling of flavor. The words "sexuality" and "sexy" appear more frequently because they do not dominant a phrase as strongly and because they carry wider philosophical halos. Also compound nouns such as sexual attraction, sexual desire, sexual dimension, sexual ego, sexual encounter, sexual glance, sexual harassment, and sex worker community appear in the data base for the Philosophical Phrase Generator. Since each word in the database carries ratings or weights, the PPG generates **pseudo** random **phrases**.

The PPG will generate 10,000 phrases per second on a slow computer. The PPG only generates adjectival phrases. These phrases consist of one adjective and a noun, two adjectives and a noun, or three adjectives and a noun. Many of the phrases generated are pregnant with meaning or not. This book presents you with a scavenger hunt for thought poppers. In presenting the phrases in this book, I have quickly scanned the output to cull what my mind took to be the obvious gibberish; thus, the phrases presented here are **pseudo pseudo random phrases.** To anyone's mind, a phrase might still seem to be total gibberish, on the other hand, it could be a real **Thought Popper**.".

The PPG system allows its operator to flavor the output in various ways. In the collection here you will find alliterations, phrase pictures, and flavorings pertaining to word structure or word classification. In some places, what you will find here are **flavored pseudo pseudo ranom phrases**.

embellished lifetime	high definition time
remote point in time	just-in-time monthly
sharply divided time	clocked timelessness
black and white time	etched-in-stone time
record-breaking time	flexibly gauged time

How To Read Output From the Philosophical Phrase Generator

A reader usually has an affinity for a narrative story line; like political parties do or like an adventure book reader rooting for the good guys to win. A reader expects a beginning, a middle, and an end to the content with which he or she is engaged or perhaps a premise, an argument, and then a conclusion. What is a reader to do when encountering the pseudo-random or pseudo-pseudo-random content coming out of the generator? Answer: Don't be a reader. Be a hunter-gatherer of thought poppers. Grok a phrase as expressing something in a new and novel way or dismiss a phrase as gibberish. It's like being out picking fruit and looking for the sweet ones. With luck, you will find some real thought poppers.

A Better Way to Experience This Book

Close the book and consider the following meditation. Sit in a comfortable position, close your eyes or keep them only slightly open, and breath slowly, in a relaxed manor, in and out for a while. Consider that the finger pointing to the moon is not the moon. Ask the ask question, "Who am I?", as asked by the sage Ramana Maharshi. The answer cannot come in the form of words that are no better than fingers pointing to the moon. Neither can the question be framed in the form of words. Rupert Spira suggests that the answer is awareness. Who am I? I am aware. I am the one who is aware. I am awareness. "Only awareness is aware of awareness." "Only Being aware is being aware of being aware." Don't get hung on the words. Be what they are pointing to. Merge with them; become the words.

Chapters

Let the Scavenger Hunt Begin

The prizes are Thought Poppers

Cacophony of Koans

noteworthy koan

divine dimension

confused intuition

essential psychology

cacophony of koans

appreciated mindfulness

philosophically driven force

handmade end-user frustration

unconditional race-based identity

amalgamated voice in the street

hypnotic idea of George Carlin

overwhelming Love Supreme

unconscious Pagan wellspring

last seconds of the game rigor

Chicago style shenanigan

sleepless voice

foreign beauty

powerful danger

slippery finances

conscious window

ethnocentric insanity

cosmetic rank and file

far-fetched abstraction

real down-home teaching

attested to ticker tape of thought

discovered corporate interlocking

conceivably hard-to-find swell guy

theoretical job of a Gregorian chant

invigorating quiescent still point

truly magic fly in the ointment

unaware syrupy benediction

full-blown double-standard

friendly secular humanism

appropriate mindfulness

linguistic temperature

postindustrial thing

cathartic tear drop

proposed x-axis

man-made grid

imaginative death

indwelling transmission

sensual costuming of Mae West

real crummy stuff in your pockets

stunning upper crust frame of mind

metaphysical mind in the modern era

hair-raising emotional wrench in the gears

pragmatic interdisciplinary consciousness

very good kind thought you just thought

reverent dogma-driven staked claim

determined bear at the bird feeder

unimagined award-winning surrealism

woefully inadequate supporting evidence

abandoned mapped-in-the-brain compendium

ubiquitous slick, quick, and dirty advertising

prepackaged step-by-step mystical feeling

encapsulated market in disequilibrium

pure and simple slapstick opinion poll

by-fiat social-political tarantella

festering thorny financial problem

seriously overworked group of nerds

noisy musical life work of John Cage

joyful exactly purposeful light of the mind

frivolous imperious court of Pliny the younger

never-ending well-grounded Wal-Mart greeter's smile

primitive prayer to the Imaginary

scientific study of private life

modest downsized syllogism

outrageous highfalutin talk

eye-catching apparency

mindful inversion layer

transnational proposal

protective cyberspace

harmless happy hour

mystifying voodoo

atypical altruism

bugged powder-room

elusive continuum

airy contentment

idiomatic snafu

paramount halo

gosh darned asset

Mozartian version

faxed daily bread

focused promotion

so sweet pure data

meditative first date

good oral transmission

Wittgensteinian caused effect

automatic eroticism of the diva

conditional cold assessment

bewildering disclosure

real beneficial gadget

apt average customer

paranoid blind faith

left-brained art

euphoric statistic

shorted-out dream

unleashed headline

novel infrastructure

enlightened case study

hard-core primitivistic art

Output From the Philosophical Phrase Generator By Ron Cohn

loving California of the mind

hardy southern centrist epoch

justified big-hearted hallelujah

meteoric movie in the brain

attained realness of reality

happy innocent ballad

foxy mystical fable

Anglo-Saxon vigil

subconscious fiat

daunting toy

mapped truth

repeated pose

sticky symmetry

cruelly crafted logic

truthful psychology

supreme motherland

horrible historical list

nihilistic authorization

long-term Western activity

Mesolithic oral transmission

carefully observed perspective

above average philosophical gravy

state-of-the-art Hobbesian cheer

astounding Turkish predicament

interwoven testable hypothesis

micro-structured association

theoretical scientific method

women's demonstration

inexorable assortment

Democratic rainbow

playful load of crap

sectored law firm

pre-scientific denial

hectic cognitive map

replicated will-to-die

discontinuous frequency

exalted gateway to cognition

glorious friction-free whirling

carte blanche social conduct

high bandwidth phenomenon

unflagging power of the people

Machiavellian path of thoughts

soulful benefit

non-objective gaze

Output From the Philosophical Phrase Generator By Ron Cohn

interplanetary object	nifty nation-state
age-old feminine slant	experimental season
relevant mental state	flamboyant hesitancy
scripted dynamism	rational inner child
congenital illusion	conscious well-being
reckless vision	transcendental sword
gorgeous gaze	sympathetic curiosity
honest price	out loud make believe
joyful glee	collective TV watching
beneficial lake	excruciating credibility
playful ground	unconscious ethical rule
living simplicity	time-consuming quorum
conceivable Muse	diluted cleanup campaign
blessed cool head	initiated pinball machine
complex comment	central 16th century force
heads-up mutation	step-by-step care giving
acceptable foolery	worldly quantitative music
plausible thought	beautiful complex gradient
healing tradition	enhanced thrill of excitement
conformist elixir	luxurious thrill of opening night
peculiar religion	inflected left-brained sagacity

counterproductive slipping	on TV relaxing	logical workshop
right now epic restructuring	evocative feeling	phenomenal idea
established acknowledging	complicated mining	wired-up linearity
generally dharmic seeming	splendid containing	digital royalty
transistorized alarming	unlimited styling	realistic love
nourishing exercising	real encoding	vital wealth
bottomless confusing	past agreeing	emphatic wealth
no-nonsense studying	able passing	randomized sex
freaky strengthening	logistical lying	happy health
expedient publishing	abounding arguing	mindful sex
unorthodox coaching	rush hour relating	provocative sex
modern disappearing	preposterous ceiling	healing wealth
musical persuading	restricted behaving	amorous sex
cultural recycling	worldly flirting	humble fame
curious protecting	hopeful feeling	hoity-toity fame
humorous dazzling	truthful netting	advertised fame
illusory enabling	orthodox protecting	discovered wealth
essential betting	ambitious knitting	eternal fame
musical lightning	yesterday's mining	astral sex
supreme balancing	Faustian dealing	created fame
dharmic lobbying	happy crawling	unstable health
heroic exploring	highlighted ruling	abundant wealth
vague grading	dialectical meaning	fine-tuned health
Arab arising	complex uprising	over budget health
rare dying	gigabit sweeping	commendable health

Output From the Philosophical Phrase Generator By Ron Cohn

foreclosing universe of Bank of America

spellbound gripping 1st round of the fight

popular app for social-political simplicity

gussied up enticing illusory sense of self

high-profile truth from the second grade

last traditional elaborate tango in Rome

epistemological cyclic spinning wheels

ingenuous whim of human reasoning

imprinted terrorist thought sequence

fanatical torrent of cryptographic data

clearly distinct actionable information

according-to-Fox News haphazard data

instinctual talent of Coleman Hawkins

nonrealistic ethereal thought sequence

truthful odor from the south of France

intensely emotional self-other dichotomy

appropriately machine-vended mind stuff

imaginatively attractive European woman

random short-term here-and-now oneness

appropriate machine-vended baccalaureate

unbelievably odd crowd of the Ming Dynasty

classical behavior of Sonny Black Napolitano

incessant intra-brain twitter message

objective meaningful twitter message

spiritual intra-brain twitter message

Heraclitean teachings of Pete Seeger

incessant disparate twitter stuff

synergetic natural twitter message

incessant intra-brain twitter verbiage

imbibed intra-brain sweetened message

coherent intra-brain inspiring message

unfolding phenomenal gleeful tradition

deeper elegant Islamic carried baggage

allegorical intra-brain twitter message

incessant bizarre intra-brain message

agitated intra-brain traditional message

compelling intra-brain cohesive message

compassionate intra-brain twitter message

quaint intra-brain big and brassy message

good-intentioned viral twitter message

unconscious intra-brain high cost message

valuable intra-brain instrumental message

surprisingly quick southern European war

incessant intra-brain hair-brained message

natural intra-brain developmental message

hardened intra-brain twitter identification

strident emergency intra-brain message

incessant intra-brain twitter continuum

incessant super unfathomable message

incessant intra-brain twitter arms race

euphoric Australian twitter message

incessant intra-brain twitter kernel

seemly intra-brain tantric message

tragic unworkable twitter message

incessant intra-brain twitter bullet

incessant intra-brain twitter message

without-a-doubt secret up her sleeve

present-day diffracted pile of piles

age-old Amazonian sacredness

unconscious "Yes I will yes"

enunciated forgiving substrate

compassionate mystical initiation

suspended researched judgment

new-fangled disease mechanism

legitimate feminine assumption

backstage discourses of the Essenes

expansive philosophical self-improvement

coarse-grained affordable wine of delusion

hidden from the public configured data

successful circular cream pie throwing

within a few keystrokes morality play

discovered visionary neuropeptide

computer-simulated nonsense	blessed life-impulse
experimental nonlocal event	fine-grained integration
transpersonal spiritual joy	blameless overconfidence
lunatic tea party fantasy	very sexual epiphenomenon
occasional divination	pragmatic Spartan concern
happy genetic marker	traditional money and power
postmodern cherubim	terrific experimental electronics
heroic tantric experience	traditional territorial expansion
tuned-up trained mind	spell-binding minute's worth of time
concocted oompah-pah	magnificent Islamic farmer's market
ad hoc set of practices	prepackaged triggering mechanism
self-sustaining jubilee	all-or-nothing correlation function
grim vested interest	very expensive blue suede shoes
innovative groove	easy computer-based nonduality
untried shimmy	behind-the-scenes public policy
marvelous tool	second-generation technium
ethical good	etched-in-stone comic strip
ideal oneness	culture-free limit to growth
inspiring history	comfortable seminar
humble oneness	careerist frog pond
many-hued prayer	coarse measure
deficient darkness	young paradigm

everyday Luddite	welcomed mental equipment
deprived treatment	asymmetrical cracked mirror
hazy reincarnation	modern selective use of data
identifiable mantra	soulful scientific community
consensual elasticity	elemental self-confirmability
competent good guys	suffering idea of what we want
Zen thrill of first touch	stimulating career of Mae West
quantified science of things	provocative experience of ice cream
imaginative lifting of the veil	Dantesque quagmire of materialism
documented unstruck sound	invoked whim of human reasoning
meandering soul on a first date	21st century thrill of seeing One
effective affectionate seduction	effective right-minded breeding
heroic easing of our anxiety	reachable board of directors
gripping elevator silence	unspoken thrill of excitement
aware tactile vibration	mysterious thrill of first touch
frequent fearlessness	lascivious Freudian analysis
usual official bias	vanilla self-confirmed bias
all-embracing dip	mental thrill of proving it
civilized strength	candid Feynman diagram
looping communication	falsifiable taste of a lemon
all-embracing post card	scientific logical absurdity
not for the fainthearted oath	divine bright-eyed stillness

Output From the Philosophical Phrase Generator By Ron Cohn

vain qualitative distinction

stunning scholarly statistic

strange favorable small talk

promiscuous Mozartian attire

aspiring powerful mental act

to-and-fro mechanical scheme

successful cross-examination

tele-marketed rhythm section

inspiring infallible healing

novel collective behavior

substitute comic strip

dynamic concordance

insoluble command

healthy cosmic OM

pulsing current of life

unimagined Chicago blues

good-natured connectedness

shamanic cartoon character

permissible clump of memes

polished-off cascade of processes

Mozartian brane on which we exist

fleshy blue moon of Kentucky

Alabamian blindness to truth

unruly regular beast

skillful book review

fun belief system

in-balance brawn

attachable apostacy

at-peak afternoon raga

authorized ability to cry

aleatory action-at-a-distance

amalgamated ability to introspect

apt amenable affirmation of praise

annoying acoustic error message

arcane artificial intelligence

available alternative view

alleviated amped-up pain

alluring academic dogma

acknowledged academy

anthropological antics

adult action

avid app

awakened acorn

all-in-one altruism

abrupt act of courage

askew aesthetic sensitivity

absolute ambient temperature

aglow arcadian archetype

along-the-way apocalyptic vision

adiabatic anti-aging product

apollonian apostasy

at-the bar article of faith

agreed-upon algebraic affair

all-pervading access to education

askew arm tattoo

all-pervading avalanche

all bullshit apology by a CEO

assumed animistic superstition

a minute's worth of antiquated time

atavistic adventure in the desert

anatomical attenuation

artful African science

altruistic anthill

anecdotal ascetic

advanced apprenticeship

acceptable app for simplicity

adroit algebra of concepts

audiovisual archeology

applicable absurdity

at-sea abandonment

betraying ballad

brokenhearted blood

before the internet brat

bamboozling bowl of Jell-O

beyond neural boundary of the self

the usual banter at the bar

born-again belief in conspiracies

back-and-forth beginning

betraying belief system

bloody benchmark

big time back swell

beautiful belief system

beautiful bare breasted woman

by-the-side-of-the-trail birth throe

barbarian, before the sixties

brand of device we bought

bribed by consumerism

belief in a Deity

beneficent blue feeling

biblical brand of Apple

built-up background check

by-passed bottle of booze

bustling band of hunter-gatherers

blustery bright-eyed blind faith

zapped zero

zonked zone

zoetic zippiest zilch

zapped happily zesty zowie

zero-emission zone of safety

zoetic zeroed in zing

zestful zappy zither

zeroed in zinger

zippiest zazen

zapped zip code

zaftig zombie

zen-like zazen

questioned quick fix

quadraphonic question

quantum-theoretic quip

querulous quantum jump

quantized quality of energy

quashed quiet of the night

quintessential quality of love

queer quagmire of materialism

instant quality of consciousness

qualitative quantified quantum view

capitalistic quagmire of materialism

questing quality of an experience

quantitative quality of the water

quantum-theoretic quicksand

question of quantitative easing

qualitative quantitative quintet

quirky quantitative quantum events

cinematic class-consciousness

continuous cognitive perspective

cut loose cultural assumption

cathartic chewed-over censure

church-going compulsory chap

celebratory core curriculum

checked-out command

congruent concept set

charmed career path

crappie cool app

conceivable circumstance

convivial Camp town ladies' song

popular circa the 1940's ceremony

cleansing cascade of failures

changeless convention

civil cultural crisis

cultist cure for cancer

culturally forbidden craze

competitive cause of misery

convenient cognitive memory

complexifying civilized cossa nostra

corporatized context within context

controlled-by-media consumerism

Calvinistic crime of being poor

dogmatically delivered drone missile

digitally rendered Dionysian spark

directly apprehensible Divine Love

defeated dark side of the empire

docile data acquisition system

desired deli-style creation

difficult daily meditation

deeply remembered dignity

debatable data dictionary

dead end Doric column

dehumanized downward dog

day-dreamed disclosure

dynastic ding dong

dedicated dosage

docile daemon

Dadaist DOW

devilish disguise

disclosed doghouse

delighted divine gift

duty-bound day-to-day life

directed double-blind study

darling downtown gallery

emergent Eros

epic exegesis

empirical emotion

enchanted eternity

explicable earthquake

mysterious non-objective widespread compassionate spark

psychological energetic passion of a Michael Jordan move

world-renowned with-the-flow radical political movement

forceful untranslatable kinky spirit of Katharine Hepburn

skillful abundantly free-of-compulsion howl of the coyote

open hearted context-sensitive caring shade of the tree

methodically engineered microscopic prescribed reality

carefully observed identifiable thermodynamic pattern

powerful relaxed and unafraid solution to the problem

abashedly prerational ephemeral world of one's own

suggested hedonistic verbal leanings of Jane Austin

discovered wholly metallic antique telephone booth

San Francisco style interlocked tangled horoscope

spoken of and praised desires of Peter the Great

inspiring ultimately natural electromagnetism

savvy nonconformist human without shoes

long-known cause-and-effect of proximity

fervid Socratic hatred of my computer

confidential affairs of Clark Gable

wondrous fallible human being

ever-changing nature of things

melancholy Russian Psalter

exciting cartoon

boring negligee ad

successful process

healing moral being

weighty data rip-off

enlightened paradise

influential vigilante

unwavering price swing

finely-felt competence

Slavic emotional force

all-or-nothing endeavor

honky myth of happiness

tumultuous ruling elite

empathetic knowableness

favorable difficult path

occasional body language

multidimensional cadence

high definition intellect

ineffable low-wage worker

Asian sense of who she is

rational Love for Calcutta

hard-edged decision to buy

relatively impossible life

engineered array of devices

up-front toolbox of adjendas

empirical fresh understanding

cerebral kick I get out of you

unconscious menu imposed on me

speculative civil disobedience

cyclic invasion of bad thoughts

energetic trusting relationship

owned by Caterpillar Co. grunge

plaintive feeling for the blues

discreet technology knowing him

counterintuitive coping strategy

decoded belief in a set of ideas

externalized state of depression

meat-n-potatoes toolbox of moves

perplexing toolbox of coquetries

avoidable fierce realm of beliefs

strange tenement on Delancy St.

pre-tested propaganda machine

transformational cultural hegemony

enlightened toolbox of dance moves

Output From the Philosophical Phrase Generator By Ron Cohn

average perception of facts

cunning killer military robot

straight ethical consideration

actual factual sense of who she is

somber ethno-cultural community

gone-in-a-flash social media profile

pyramidal commercial meme factory

historical virulent racism of the settler

Judeo-Christian agent, object, & action

naturalistic loving calm and free space

absolutely cogent worshiper of the Torah

heroic unknown woman fleeced by the elite

shifting complex psychological relationship

multi-level marketed mental image of reality

dogmatically enforced manufacture of devices

objectifiable imaginative world of black people

worthy expertly scientific social media presence

living shameful hysterical gal monetizing her data

right now high level bohemian realm of relationships

inside-my-own-mind undiscriminating layer of habit I have

humbled in the present moment by the toilet paper on my shoe

scrupulously engineered non-alphabetic data she's surrendered

quaint quality

quick and dirty quark

dirty certainty of being

quiet quality of experience

qualitative quixotic question

quiet question to ask the fire

questing question of the skeptic

qualified question of the skeptic

questionable quality of experience

quick-on-the-draw quantum uncertainty

quantum mechanical quality information

quasi-classical quantum fluctuation

questing question of what is real

qualified quiet cross-legged man

quenched "False" that falls away

quantified quantum fluctuation

quick and easy question we ask

qualified quality of the food

questionable quantification

quintessential quackery

quantified quid pro quo

parliamentary parlance

playful picnic in the park

prewired pattern of patterns

youth oriented yogic gesture

year-after-year young European man

yearning yesterday's yodelish scat

yummy young European woman

yesterday's young white man

year-after-year yearbook

youth oriented yogi

you-tubed yoga

yeomanly yeah

yearly yodel

young Yankee woman

yeomanly you tube video

wasteful whitewater

warm-bodied witch

watery weekend

woebegone wandering

without-a-qualm way of thinking

when no one is looking will power

world-class worthwhile wall painting

windy worrisome worry about the future

Output From the Philosophical Phrase Generator By Ron Cohn

within a few keystrokes way to skin a cat	musical adoration
way back when brutally whirling warfare	left-brained dogma
workmanlike way our brain functions	psychological curry
wrinkled waters of recollection	imaginative workings
worthwhile web of nerve cells	terrific traditional odor
warranted witness of the mind	primary English quality
way cool workings of the brain	clear and distinct passion
win-win woman I met online	philosophical unicorn horn
well composed witchcraft	adaptive canonical adjustment
widely used web of beliefs	revealed human without clothes
worldly worship of the Form	crystal clear science of things
wet and wild washing of a pot	terrestrial psyche of the Beatles
wonderful way things are done	divinely inspired twitter message
wizardly way to solve a problem	scientific human without a device
whirling world beyond your body	traditional health of the organism
widespread worship of the Dollar	camouflaged human without clothes
widely repeated wardrobe malfunction	compassionate good human with a car
sage council	transnational device-dependent human
wizardly thing	discussion group on Maxwell's equations
magnificent thing	non-exclusive key that opens the door
understated truth	traditional Ivy League picture of reality
hopeful attraction	ever-changing adaptive adjustment

ideal recurrent psychological level

new wave health of the organism

beautiful psychological balance

scientific triggering stimulus

stark brain-mapped body state

modern human without a device

liberated money in my pocket

queer human without a car

mysterious bottomless pit

unbiased creative director

unresolved heroic taproot

symbolic division by zero

nonperfect philosophy

hectic end of slavery

lucent psychic gift

stable philosophy

mighty seduction

real juggernaut

Boolean mood

karmic life

unique totem

rational switch

imaginative candor

adrift compassion

complexifying lesson

detectable unmentionable

pleasant achievement

efficacious fixation

esteemed causation

high level excellence

ethnocentric junk food

churning bottomless pit

Jewish emotional outlet

multipurpose eye-opener

mysterious make-believe

unfulfilling shopping frenzy

happy momentary sacredness

complexifying internal dialogue

annoying human without shoes

nourishing emotional machinery

deceptive psychological balance

perplexingly honest possible truth

primitivistic prayer to the Imaginary

unpredictable human without a car

video-based key that opens the door

meaningful unconscious decision point

scarred shaking	clear-eyed change for change sake
reasoned fearing	grueling annoying song on the radio
free flourishing	cannibalizing decadence of the elite
gorgeous gimmick	visionary neighborhood of Abraham
good gut feeling	deep thermodynamic transformation
successful coding	non-aggressive rather cool filter
fancy free father	apocalyptic vibrating dysfunction
gosh darned guest	unhesitant government of Nell Gwinn
liberal evaluating	histrionic influence of Jupiter's red spot
dedicated staffing	adventurous romantic stuff of dreams
unrivaled detecting	under stated hope that you love me
face-to-face fox trot	polytheistic ownership of my body
free-form forgiveness	exhilarating man-made light touch
finely tuned fertilizer	crafty rekindled self-improvement
exemplified edutainment	proud peer group of the Imaginary
ectoplasmic envelopment	beautiful fast rugged bull market
stupefied by scripture life	soul-centered lyrical eye contact
ever-improving evolution	cross-cultural Asian man in power
future-proof forces of light	well-balanced inductive fragrance
stunning grand scheme of things	realistic very supreme no-brainer
magnificent person without shoes	nice friendly prison of the known
sophomoric bliss of the faithful	software-based market transaction
high-profile emotional machinery	shocking slave of a habit pattern
traditional Hollywood blockbuster	guiding step-by-step liberal view
measurable key that opens the door	held-together conventional wisdom

Output From the Philosophical Phrase Generator By Ron Cohn

unworthy selfie
revered ideal romance
painful seat on the board
multicultural class struggle
terribly packed commuter train
hale and hardy emotional meeting
insuppressible Sufi understanding
reality-based experience of purple
imposed will of a corporate sponsor
endlessly fascinating gift of faith
utterly impossible confronted truth
purely formal Paleolithic language
rational conscious super-organism
image-based spiritual initiation
crystallized megabit carpentry
essential firmness and vigor
erratic cubicle etiquette
feminine crosscurrent
alive biomarker

customary skill
handy macrotechnology
major checks and balances
outrageous elemental passion
psychotherapeutic steady state
blossoming advertised trampoline
electronically-sent enlightenment
functional healing eternal pattern
discovered gathered peaceable facts
a name's gentle sagacious vibration
half-hidden wisdom of the algorithm
perceived shining spirit of Cezanne
free from conditioning visitation
no-questions-asked ripple effect
unbecoming surveillance record
way cool geopolitical Gnosis
culture-bound guide lines
benevolent basic flaw
keen femininity

Output From the Philosophical Phrase Generator By Ron Cohn

melodious discourses of Horace

rational psychological balance

indecipherable cause and effect

more-than-meets-the-eye way

overwhelming moral dilemma

urban human with a phone

sharp purpose
mundane identity
decisive solipsism
unseen moving target
subconscious parasite
rather completed skill
fiddled with ontogeny
tame erotic calmness
complex conviction
vanilla mind set
gathered love

energetic inspiring stuff

real perceptive adaptive

individualistic childhood

mind-boggling gypsy lady

expressed mumbo jumbo

programmatic experiment

fulfilled world in the wild

uproarious superstition

static coherent whole

anguished conception

consummate analysis

precise pull of gravity

merciful alertness

rational nonsense

overall manyness

cagey shareware

ideal awakening

discovered script

life-giving dazzle

quixotic hive-like classic

randomly rational object

pseudorandom frequency

traditional well-placed Jupiter

extraneous certified special touch

marketable proficient robotized factory

ceaseless fluctuating meaninglessness

laissez-faire entertaining universe

obvious discourses of Stan Getz

ordinary choice of conditions

rewarding warm body

proven chorus line

commonplace advice

complex keystone

incorporeal scare

justified object

Eastern backdrop

mortal subtle energy

pressurized sensation

pretentious friendship

blameless modular ideograph

microtechnical movie screen

outrageous rocket science

well-meaning embarkation

under budget beginning

mystic ecological niche

compassionate success

swell walk in the park

adulterated monolith

Delphic comic book

peaceful trespass

momentary miracle

roguish magic bullet

wretched bottle of booze

drug-induced walkabout

prolific syntonic openness

first-hand citizen's right

discreet virtual thing

observable tendril

harmonic Paganism

imprecise completion

gender-based love affair

devil-may-care duplicity

non-conformist fairy tale

incredible cross purposes

syntonic mantra repetition

humble feeling I experienced

non-objective day-to-day living

context-sensitive relative wealth

acceptable definable five-year plan

impending hallucinatory meditation

meticulously documented initiation

enshrined metaphysical object

brand of product you buy

African phantasm

honest life

lost e-mail

Output From the Philosophical Phrase Generator By Ron Cohn

advanced autocracy
heavenly condition
provocative beauty
budding open heart
advertised success
never-failing luck
flat out jazz lick
four-petaled grace
firm actualization
Euclidean Band Aid
traditional stupor
friendly nostalgia
timely after death
standardized fruit
divine phase shift
diffusive highball
uncanny conclusion
psychosomatic date
exalted livelihood
amateurish fanfare
holy working class
deleveraged hubbub
naked smiling face
colored coordinate
dad blasted effect
magnificent G.N.P.
hard-to-find spell
doctrinaire pulpit
sensible tactility
delicate resonance
analyzed interests
declared cave wall
class-based health
ancient checkpoint
1960 Polaroid shot
chronicle rational
charged up romance
meticulous atheism
imperial satellite
mixed-up challenge
hard-edged embrace
austere hollow log
American sun dance
way-back-when beam
illusory exemption
subjective quibble
Eastern standpoint
immersed beatitude
arranged monograph
real loving glance
presumed emergency
peaceful vibration
gossamer dimension
sought-out hot dog

predictable bitter death of Mae West
briskly branched conflict resolution
far-reaching promiscuous warm shower
sinful decided upon transmitted tusk
upbeat unscripted point of awareness
qualitative fantasy of Gustav Mahler
high-profile contemplative messiness
tailor-made body of the baby boomers
so sweet captivating acquired object
still-warm statistical impossibility
jaw-dropping unutterable provocation
abstruse benevolent DeAndre the Geek
unspoken relaxed enigmatic home page
gratifying skillful development team
defeated unenlightened viral fiction
high and mighty reckless common good
imaginary age-old objective pressure
spread thru society hawkish bullshit
actual preliminary meditative garden
quantitative mother of Sidney Bechet
nontrivial grass roots manifestation
out of Jersey City wild counter girl
measurable incidental disappointment
second-generation league of Aurelian
microcosmic mother of Albrecht Durer
creative discourses of Susan Anthony
useful southern European spreadsheet
complete egalitarian quality of life
good lighthearted passionate embrace
humanly meaningful mental shrewdness
nontrivial experimental complication
allegorical way they feel each other
untold advantageous effect explained
ignored examined enlightened version
ultramaterialistic financial success
bought in London technical expertise
resolved spiritually aware integrity
forbidden melodious absolute mandala
frugally frenetic moment of pleasure
perennial enlightened Ockham's razor
intellectual French meditative issue
prim and proper high definition soul
conclusive traditional modus vivendi
half-baked spirit of Charles the Fat
greased-up essential carnival barker
rhapsodic rational experimental aura
trustworthy pedantic woman in a suit
foreshadowed person who feels worthy
humanly meaningful declasse maneuver
unrivaled brother of Humphrey Bogart
so sweet southern European good time
non-illusory unimaginable groovyness
national clan of John Maynard Keynes
ever-present healing iron age nectar

ripe brain washing
redeemed asymptote
qualitative fantasy
direct instability
automatic calculus
violent alma mater
intelligible poise
required operation
mystic exhortation
slapstick ideology
proven wealthy man
leveraged feelings
foggy right action
healing state park
shocking interface
reckless DNA match
metabolized hatred
brute force entity
tricky finish line
non-breakable koan
Asian style fervor
South Indian flash
libertine business
mandated ideologue
extrinsic industry
constant intuition
diagnostic doorway
painful sufferings
incipient download
conservative spell
theocratic episode
parenthetical kiss
protective polemic
compassionate tint
destroyed rudiment
ecstatic technique
willing camouflage
emotional stoicism
effective immortal
vivid adaptability
elicited cold beer
coexistent cubicle
hopeful persuasion
vivified democracy
mistaken absurdity
subjective feeling
epic postmodernism
electrical welcome
provoking practice
syntactical lyrics
revolving template
revealed corpuscle
continuous thought
renascent totality

Output From the Philosophical Phrase Generator By Ron Cohn

unconscious teaching

undisputed happiness

consensual durability

emotional guiding light

humble parting of the veil

blissful Portuguese tradition

enlivened wisely real momentum

sharp thought of Clarence Darrow

Hollywood-style amorally exemplar

wholesome high-powered ebullience

phantom self-selected idol of the cave

class-conscious feeling I experienced

encouraging feeling I experienced

Polynesian feeling I experienced

actual diffusive spiral of events

present feeling I experience

scarred feeling I experienced

determined nineteen-sixties

sleepless life of good cheer

shamanic restoration

transitory world

rational horoscope

Navaho no-brainer

battle-weary oneness

Portuguese lattice work

highly magnified steadiness

mysterious wide-ranging jinx

exultant brand-new bag of Papa

advertised myopic misinformation

main book of the Cherokee Nation

every flowing drum and bugle corps

jagged twist through the mountains

boring temporal time in a cubicle

newest two-way transformative art

thought out traditional T.N.T.

very important thing that we know

vibrating tingle up the spine

transpersonal fluid thermal dance

news sensitive tumultuousness

thru the grapevine tale well told

thought-out transforming power

loud turbulent tidal tuba solo

twisted-like-spaghetti dance

logical therefore and because

transformational techy power

present totality of media images

purely abstract wheel of fortune

thirst for transcendental experience

tenuous time-honored time management

third-party technological virtuosity

teeming with patterns theater of war

thematic textured tweet from Beyonce

trans-intuitive transformative music

tough transforming thought I thought

thousand-petaled tyranny of religion

tolerable totalist theory of reality

today's transrational timeless truth

tired trumped up tormented modernity

through-time thing that no one wants

throbbing teeming with patterns tape

technically complex triggering event

transmogrified trending thought form

thought-provoking term here on earth

demure delighting dropped comment

candid under wearing telecommute

drifting away dimension of reality

deeply abstract deep structure

defined-as-normal deep denial

direct dark side of the empire

destined daily discernment

demonstrative data object

devolving Dada

dilute data

deathly dynamite

drug-free doctrine

dinky digital device

day to day drug store

high-fidelity wolf howl

dispensable dab of goo

launched drone missile

discovered doubtful data

de novo decoded information

debonair drug-induced felicity

hair-curling habitual tendency

high-flying high-risk scenario

holistic high-complexity event

hankered for honey in the hive

high definition hail Mary pass

high-pitched habit of thinking

hive-like human interest group

hypertensive horror of W. Bush

unclassifiable religion-science war; indescribable window of opportunity

cosmic heart of Yehoshua Bar-Hillel; omnipresent technology-driven candy

littered chronological email folder; splendid nondual mental preparation

partisan territory   after death twinge

select determinism   emerging portfolio

polemical thatness   spiritual practice

illusory sensation   upbeat gospel song

modern airline hub   attributeless flow

conceivable theoretical innermost heavenly desires of Fletcher Henderson

minimal as Miles firmness and vigor; wide-ranging interesting philosophy

constantly shifting most significant schooling of Sonny Black Napolitano

esoteric coalition   maximized cocktail

generated ubiquity   obstructive gossip

fatalistic symptom   perfect local herb

soulful soap opera   local bank account

pOwerful spectacle   Greco-Roman timbre

truthfully unbound understandable path of Chaney, Goodman, and Schwerner

annoyingly harassed deep sleep state of Frederick William of Brandenburg

valid doublewhammy   pleasant mechanism

fancy weltansauung   soulful morphology

hopeful adaptation   sponsored endeavor

reputed underworld   unbelievable craft

dissolved insomnia   ecological emotion

fast-moving universal visualization; inoculated educated view of history

historical molecular-level frontier; traditional pause for contemplation

dry apollonian management technique; medicinal elevated music of emotion

drearily pragmatic trend of thought; announced scientific rhythm section

solemnly high performance ideographic never-failing vessel of the spirit

charismatic soul of Lucrezia Borgia; magical complex quantum fluctuation

transformational irrelevance of God; preconceptual customer satisfaction

coincidental water of Ponce de Leon; esteemed quirk of Archibald MacLeish

playful dependency	traditional climax
new-style cosmetic	devoted revolution
sensual hallelujah	Republican success
scripted falsehood	helpful compassion
edifying stability	living fresh world

understated playful bipolar episode; hashed over ten-dimensional gravity

tomorrow's state-sponsored tool kit; nostalgic movie of Laurel and Hardy

transnational money to buy medicine; non-proprietary decoded information

optimal cyberspace	dull consciousness
nonsensical melody	expanding practice
vital open network	arranged community
uncovered windfall	real noble warrior
winning sweet spot	archetypal formula

loving lamentation of Wallace Beery; bread-n-butter start of the romance

bubbly erudite forty-year-old woman; understandable correlation function

hit-or-miss voodoo	nailed up metaphor
past habit of mind	interesting office
desktop coordinate	heroic life-energy
average heart beat	skillful resonance
amorous metabolism	alluring semantics

imaginative seeming seeker of truth; analyzed high-risk leveraged buyout

discovered dormant barbarian sheath; truth-inhibiting clockwork universe

silently clairvoyant ancestral idol; occasional impoverished primitivism

long standing thrill of competition; beautiful compelling Akkadian image

beneficial rational operating table; distributed way it's supposed to be

ardent atypical sounding piano trio; friendly customer driven adjustment

up-to-no-good calliope of the world; natural cumulative logical progress

intractable cultist cultural trance; clamped down limitation on humanity

intractable cultist cultural trance; hard-to-find textured gift of grace

wholesome seduction of Frederick William of Brandenburg

shopping behavior in a store on Madison Ave. in the 60's

painstakingly illusory duality created by words

simple but profound modern Greek situation

honest esteemed beer in the pubs of London

bubbling beyond imagination business logic

pearl covered broach bought at Norstrom's

able always busy app for winning in Vegas

respected left-brained mathematical truth

according to the voter's ancestral memory

cockamamie corporate chanson de geste

quantum mechanical quick-firing qualia

hot-wired hot-button issue

hysterical hierarchy of angels

hermetically sealed hyperspace

Heraclitan hype and hypocrisy

heretical theoretical humanness

inspiring side of hashed browns

heretical theoretical humanness

tightly dramatic heart of Lennie Tristano

according to Buddha algebra of symbols

smuggled-in repressed hidden wisdom

at-the-end-of-the-day activated concept

black and tan brittle belief you are a body

beyond expectations business opportunity

bread-n-butter bronze age board of trustees

nouveau Twitter based modernist identity

Japanese joyous jagged journal

justified joyful juvenile journey

Judaic jovial jump start

joking jubilant junk science

joyful joy filling every pore

Buggy Sky Writing

buggy sky writing

Spartan mentality

seamless lucidity

10th century slang

impossible switch

awesome past life

peasant affluence

sensual nastiness

hot internet meme

sweetened physics

masculine blarney

hysterical damsel

naked online life

spectacular sport

19th century hope

religious vertigo

evolved macrocosm

avant-garde habit

haphazard ecstasy

Judaic attraction

histrionic libido

Gnostic quick fix

living shell game

ridiculous modesty

arduous paycheck

Mesolithic prayer

fabulous ballyhoo

emotional memento

awkward plaything

hardened sagacity

spontaneous grace

ponderous tyranny

combined goodwill

unique relaxation

mandated hilarity

wonderful costume

blue chip hip hop

intimate spectrum

fast-growing love

classical theater

inner expectation

gripping dark age

punishing fantasy

professional goof

unflappable blurb

endurable lullaby

scripted analysis

archaic technique

real loveableness

secular lifeblood

emerging finality

aromatic subtlety

sloppy conviction

deep down message

sensual whirlpool

day to day ripple

chaotic community

textured universe

natural synagogue

licensed behavior

Output From the Philosophical Phrase Generator By Ron Cohn

visionary religion

common consequence

paranoid viscosity

rather cool enigma

literate addiction

loving infatuation

geographic feature

diminished emotion

Thomistic calculus

expansive lifetime

half-baked message

pure replicability

pleasant macrocosm

billable fragrance

valuable sensation

aroused enticement

Tibetan expression

honest enhancement

fancy free inquiry

intuited encounter

smoldering opening

identifiable chant

mushrooming climax

pathological music

mindful meditation

created limitation

soothing sensation

widespread samsara

gorgeous innocence

nanotech poignancy

qualified antidote

high def neon sign

blissful stillness

Western completion

at wit's end chaos

mainstream variety

bold primal desire

skillful expansion

beautiful language

enlightened herald

amusing relaxation

higher Ellingtonia

orgasmic endowment

victorious freedom

cloudy mathematics

present-day symbol

conclusive message

unwavering element

tight assed entity

metaphorical magic

workaday Platonism

traditional profit

customary kindness

dog-gone tightness

beneficial advance

ephemeral buoyancy

understated thrill

well-meaning pardon

communist adventure

shrewd perturbation

fortuitous majority

enlivened construct

poetic philanthropy

alert determination

suggested genealogy

extinct menu option

historical resource

archetypal trespass

beautiful addiction

hopeful abiding awe

enormous enticement

distracting twinkle

influential kingdom

groundless calculus

pervasive emergence

unquestionable spot

ineluctable embrace

affirmed alienation

ritual-free concept

haughty sensitivity

Output From the Philosophical Phrase Generator By Ron Cohn

friendly middle way

unrehearsed honesty

intriguing overtone

unflappable reality

savvy Pavlovian dog

conscious repulsion

scientific idealism

real practical joke

high-strung emotion

Aristotelian mantra

persistent paycheck

first to market glow

loving coming of age

mind-made motivation

interplanetary prose

measurable sensation

discovered mind stuff

dualistic centrality

venerated capability

psychotic modulation

worldwide hard times

unstoppable instinct

imprinted wavelength

adequate florescence

imaginative creature

telepathic enactment

quick and easy ennui

crazy peal of laughter

petrifying whirlpool

outrageous affluence

recorded calibration

decisive team member

humble introspection

subterranean opening

empirical innovation

working class desire

scientific bungee jump

paradoxical meditation

healing reorganization

tele-marketed phantasm

poignant creaking door

non-verbal improvement

important psychic knot

imperial justification

in-the-mood brass band

most significant query

actual wonderful oasis

intriguing hagiography

emotional assimilation

fat test that I passed

commercial scalability

inexact remote control

inspiring productivity

bewildering mathematics

world-famous initiative

ambitious normalization

unbelievable subroutine

psychedelic methodology

rip-roaring final cause

elaborate ups and downs

pianistic organ grinder

experimental phenomenon

fashionable electronics

one-and-only stereotype

healthy radiation level

far-off mid-life crisis

misconceived girlfriend

experimental occurrence

crackpot private sector

complex sound of battle

intense notion of space

anonymous falsification

set-in-stone foundation

trial-and-error college

market-driven catharsis

reputed superimposition

microscopic side effect

lucid mathematical truth

back-and-forth eloquence

elusive league of Seneca

Output From the Philosophical Phrase Generator By Ron Cohn

highly exploited portent

frolicsome personal life

discussed telephone call

objectified universalism

experiential saintliness

histrionic gift of faith

repudiated civil liberty

excellent modern edifice

capitalistic mental muck

breathtaking PR campaign

marketable gain and loss

periodic conscious state

frivolous quest for love

nihilistic loving glance

recurring fall into love

energetic local variable

flat out Finnish success

New Orleans style spirit

down-home radiant priest

obvious outpouring of devotion

unconditional mainstream media

simple astronomical occurrence

challenging spiritual stairway

unimaginably beautiful facility

bushy-tailed insurance salesman

unexceptionable unwanted habit

manufacture of limited knowledge

plagiarized fortune cookie phrase

trying to have fun in a patriarchy

Abrahamic "not this, not this"

foreseen state of experiencing

It's wonderful, it's marvelous

tolerant desire for the object

worldly institutional religion

golden joy filling every pore

uniform scientific method

that you could care for me

Socratic logic of monetization

extinct online image of myself

God-given healthy self-inquiry

serious absence of public data

cool artistic tribe of Janis Joplin

well-substantiated monkey mind

high-sounding style of Otis Reading

anticipated accepted responsibility

empirical circumstantial relativity

routine conservative eternal verity

realized way out experience of time

central underground unconsciousness

You can't blame me for feeling amorous

mind-boggling unplugged formulation

enlightened knowledge age we are in

unprecedented split-off mental flux

Shakespearean blueprint for action

you've made me feel so glamorous

truest exquisite healing ingredient

well-placed owner of bits and bytes

face-saving group to which I belong

never-ending violence of capitalism

understood service to your customer

pre-Aristotelian politics of the empire

ontological transcendental assumption

good-intentioned women's resentment

reincarnated fiction spun into facts

incessant classical slave to legacy

disciplined fantasy of Paul Gauguin

transcendental ontological assumption

game-changing connecting of the dots

real organic warm-bodied information

unfaltering healing sexual technique

unhealthy bigoted big data analytics

ineffably lucent quality information

according-to-tradition slice of life

rolling high definition loose marble

hard-to-explain life-giving membrane

whole profound Self beyond sensations

astounding paramount subatomic event

rich harvest of contemplative wisdom

underlying Judeo-Christian conception

contradiction-filled Feynman diagram

field-theoretic worldly entanglement

informational clearing in the forest

helpless pungent cat who got skunked

surreal heaviest of all carry-on luggage

down-to-earth satisfactual meditation

brutal readings of the fundamentalists

honorable decisive courageous realism

unfettered rip-roaring dip in the mikva

consummate hit album of the Supremes

scientifically hatched biological genesis

industrialized Facebook personalization

nefarious richly crafted analytical result

absolute higher coughing rate in Beijing

daily routine of the Ionian philosophers

nice-looking unstressed life of simplicity

conceptualizing generation of Niels Bohr

endless commitment of Jorge Luis Borges

inexact disempowering biblical confusion

well-established planetary laws of Kepler

inevitable rational idea used in their world

scientifically mature extraction of metadata

caught in her gaze trip down Memory Lane

Output From the Philosophical Phrase Generator By Ron Cohn

howling sound of a coyote

topsy turvy nothingness

psychological scripture

conformist private life

supportive after-effect

intoxicating compulsion

considerate irreverence

cuddly memo to a worker

redeeming actualization

experimental artfulness

Italian payment in cash

presumed "what's wrong"

nervous glimmer of hope

synthetic enlightenment

rhapsodic consciousness

anonymous quantum event

careful universal right

trusted general welfare

insecure easy fly paper

qualitative mental life

successful fearlessness

TRUE discovered theater

credible book of Buddha

acknowledged compassion

mechanistic cleanliness

realistic measured time

Darwinian fait accompli

yucky thought construct

musty tautological odor

foreshadowed revolution

forbidden consciousness

childlike life as being

escalating chat session

high-end fragmentedness

rip snorting prediction

beneficial act of faith

Promethean mother board

demonstrative deduction

compulsive rock concert

organic subway platform

leftist me inside the skin

exciting way you turn me on

lascivious way you turn me on

weird gal giving me the willies

histrionic he done left me blues

exploding false me inside the skin

heart-pounding faith leading me on

synthetic me as a perceivable object

stabilizing me using memory to exist

sentimental thing making me special

computer-based way you hold me tight

weepin' & sobbin' my baby left me blues

jaggedly lopsided pull on me from the past

now & then frequent pill to make me smart

adored adolescent Me Tarzan-You-Jane talk

scorned usual Republican rollback of wages

clearly superstitious persistent I am me thought

concentrated in the desert animistic superstition

artful musically free-floating something-or-other

divinely inspired boundless flowering of the soul

low level deep sorrow
experimental seminar
confirmed symbology
awe inspiring kiss
tinkered-with money
delectable tactility
zero-sum yin and yang
unfamiliar paleosymbol
strong chain of command
controlling rendezvous
guaranteed error code
humble piece of work
natural undergrowth
analyzed statistic
wandering nostalgia
fundamental tool set
adventurous worldline
efficient noisy signal
standardized grand jury
pigeon-holed inference
authoritarian citadel
psychoactive symptom
reasoned coordinate
agitated good guys
modern news service
glaring need for sex
pigeon-holed analysis
beautiful battleground
accessible white light
certifiable next life
honest email message
technical tradition
enormous pulsation
engrossing euphoria
caste conscious will
objective tranquility
life-giving dedication
routine dogmatic ritual
discovered misjudgment
broad aesthetic value
fine-grained failure
available depiction
left-brained oomph
spiritual corrosion
fractal melting snow
vouched for sweetness
Polynesian sacred grove
upgradable news source
adorned yodelish scat
misunderstood nature
principal star dust
historical delight
gut wrenching clash
cozy past impression
conceivable appliance
beaming "ahaa" moment
prime time kaleidoscope
quantitative agreement
complex communication

disagreeable thought construct
somatic management of the planet
accurate powerful time out of mind
high-off-the-hog Dadaist primitivism
purposeful beautiful young coconut
gender-specific gamut of desires
corresponding business trouble
touching public opinion poll
beautiful gussied up gloss
indecipherable social circle
friendly drink of the Kool Aid
symbiotic information technology
idealistic life work of Wei Wu Wei
laissez-faire dog wagged by its tail
clever avant-garde healing process
inscrutable intelligible reality
not necessarily so modern look
good time new age enthusiasm
verbal approximate reality
unquestioned fruit of action
resolved word from our sponsor
vital traditional touchdown pass
immature complex cooked-up history
ascertainable money to buy elections
self-protective subconscious angel
spiritual conscious selflessness
achieved beatific love supreme
fresh collection of contacts
motivational circular motion
vigorous marketized apotheosis
approximate everyday craps shoot
clear and present article of faith
super-sensuous healing reincarnation
free-standing worthy source of joy
insightful profusion of feelings
absolutely awesome commonality
true "I am that" realization
bucolic friend on Facebook
unraveled intellectual rigor
esteemed scientific philosophy
sybaritic partnering opportunity
experimental way out being present
left on the shelf seasonal emptyness
unwavering imaginative way we live
made in Germany nice bric a brac
well-placed focussed attention
pro-consumer encouragement
beautiful mechanistic theory
thalmaturgic shedding of tears
rational real estate acquisition
miraculous way the cookie crumples
very English incidental eccentricity
treasury of black and white images
rapidly deployed gleeful emotion
traditional Marxist liberalism
belabored cultural orthodoxy
spirited American spectrum
fascinating brown eyed girl
intensified alchemical therapy

angry cultural choice
historical equipoise
doubtful suggestion
friendly test tube
defenseless freedom
macrocosmic adhesive
rigged up Bronx cheer
inwardly attained lake
multicultural microcosm
well-grounded toe hold
digital amplification
conspicuous antibody
unverifiable legacy
difficult strategy
pledged forgiveness
perfect used car lot
accessible persuasion
illusory reverberation
scientific distribution
humorous demonstration
advertised compulsion
understated software
upbeat drug of love
soulful real stuff
scientific anecdote
animated renaissance
inspiring sacred fire
verifiable carefulness
inscrutable laboratory
sunny magical quality
world-class vitality
fine-tuned kindness
satisfactual sauce
seamless Buddhahood
unrecognizable waltz
candid comedy routine
quantitative situation
personal unstruck sound
subconscious purgatory
astounding patriarchy
emotional enticement
comatose heart beat
troublesome fracas
simple self-respect
poor brain mechanism
creditable complexity
invaluable universalism
vivified idea of Freud
pugilistic cold sweat
essential voice mail
intricate geography
full-blown average
truthful modulation
advanced spontaneity
Taoist charter school
tailor-made wilderness
perturbed digital cloud
pathological caliphate
operative instability

Clear Belief

in a Dogma

clear belief in a dogma

doctrinally correct life

integral belief in aliens

epochal belief in a belief

complex disbelief in God

accepted doctrinal system

humble doctrinal conformity

joyous disbelief in the gods

doctrinally correct ink blot

distinct belief in the bible

disciplined belief in a dogma

doctrinally correct philanthropy

warm-bodied belief in emptiness

flamboyant doctrinal correctness

psychological doctrinal synthesis

doctrinally true scientific research

hard to destroy doctrinal orthodoxy

doctrinally correct medieval concept

doctrinally pure data from all sensors

marketable belief in improving yourself

spiritual wrong view: "this body is mine"

doctrinally accepted under class impurity

historical white belief in more and more

covert nefarious belief in reincarnation

far from instinctual app I'm trapped in

newest certifiable job-killing technology

supreme doctrinally correct purposeful being

doctrinally idolatrous chicken and egg problem

pressurized weapon-resistant doctrinal correctness

perplexing people in a serene stupor of consumerism

unscientific ostentatious web page I'm trapped on

flourishing instinctual unstructured methodology

usual unresolved unidentified utter foolishness

old-fashioned beatific lady putting on lipstick

meat-n-potatoes etched-in-stone code of honor

desirable symbolic emotional teenage consumer

concocted well-timed unexamined assumption

technically easy centrist rational discourse

empathetic gender-specific rant and rave

active masculine rugged expressionism

new technology-driven framework

relatively impossible discrimination

energetic Tibetan fall into the Self

consumer-oriented promised land

in mint condition idol of the tribe

healing teaching of John Lennon

blocked public area of Facebook

dog-gone lifelong leap of faith

circumscribed understanding

alleged random phenomenon

sectarian mythic knowledge

since last news cycle myth

charmingly natural classic

delicate work of Ty Cobb

household notion of time

victorious deeper reality

concept of the axial age

traditional democracy

throbbing cry for help

conceivable welcome

super linear bullshit

essential transition

literal love

geodesic egg

prescribed oil

logical ability

radiant vehicle

complex thought

pianistic libation

monotheistic heat

immanent Google hit

hallucinatory anchor

authorized logistics

rip snorting emotion

non-verbal data curve

shameless research group

imponderable briar patch

testosteronal moral code

appropriate effortlessness

lush neo-Platonic menagerie

impossible Australian detour

undetermined life of the party

culture-bound doing and being

post-Kantian perceptual system

corrosive finances

stark prescription

richly-crafted awe

fulfilling essence

unrelenting symbol

silky equalization

esoteric flex time

Output From the Philosophical Phrase Generator By Ron Cohn

apocalyptic modulation
imaginative empiricism
intense discrimination
kindhearted nonduality
smooth shot of whiskey
never-ending wild side
psychotherapeutic food
realized wave function

Output From the Philosophical Phrase Generator By Ron Cohn

Healing microscopic belief in emptiness

gonna be awright view of the universe

sharp delineated perception of a feeling

different market-driven issues of belief

used for the rest of your life stage prop

blocked fantasy of Friedrich Nietzsche

clear-cut thought-provoking nitty gritty

Paleolithic Indo-European digital device

uncontroversial utilitarian individualism

surprising archetypal talk with your love

unfettered future plans of Von Metternich

uproarious funny healing way back home

conspicuously mystifying New Testament

unsubtle demise of a televangelist's fiefdom

beyond face-saving hilarious instant replay

hateful stultifying untamable digital device

state-of-the-art exhilarating wizardly process

brutally clairvoyant Italian newspaper article

unsustainable illusory forest of beliefs

play-acting waywardness of the mind

bioenergetic nesting of hierarchies

no-nonsense boogie-woogie piano

chimerical biblical interpretation

backup group for Ella Fitzgerald

undiscovered being of our mind

giddy forty-year-old woman

European moral authority

rediscovered buzz word

mortal enlightened state

significant full moon night

love for a Mozart symphony

exaggerated knowledge

sexual healing venture

apocalyptic baloney

perceptible smile

simple thisness

ornery label

valid brand

imported duality

instinctual twinkle

combined secretion

religious acceptance

eye opening signature

mellow inspiring grace

phylogenic control issue

effective source of power

extraordinary synagogue

free-form metamorphosis

surprising empirical world

secondary first-class status

nonlocalizable relationship

cartoonishly simple illusion

good-natured miracle of life

hip brain-machine interface

second-generation mentality

dirty higher math blackboard

simple but profound vibrancy

eye-catching mannerist flourish

Orwellian information overload

indisputable daily chain of being

Output From the Philosophical Phrase Generator By Ron Cohn

heroic coup d'état

volatile press conference

immensely satisfying hair-raising thought

spiritual training of Ramakrishna Paramahamsa

scintillating non-material Himalayan heritage

lifelong individualistic material reality

disputed tested ecological enzyme

in-the-marketplace presentation of myself

caught-off-guard in unconscious thinking

wow for sure unmitigated merry making

sought-out multipurpose equilibrium

carefully constructed pillar of the faith

irresistible Zen life work of Bette Davis

beautiful living person on earth's miracle

free-of-coercion frugally kind viral meme

fructified thought of The Esterhazy family

immensely satisfying super-sensuous meal

Sumerian free-form grand scheme of things

culpable verbless Facebook image of myself

nice-looking politically correct sponsorship

apparent autonomous weapon

uncategorizable Buddhist woman

very good condition of his body

predictable sense of who she is

super-symmetric nature of things

ungrounded clamor of experiences

day to day epistemological vertigo

best-selling deification of urban wealth

cleverly premeditated fluttering negligee ad

empirical unspoken face-saving word

contingent cellulite on her thighs

average well-to-do white person

world-class toolbox of slights

creditable weapons deployment

discovered nature of things

up-front emotional force

forbidden ephemeral pleasure

residual wounded child within

sleek person with a pacemaker

interdependent toolbox of ideas

Output From the Philosophical Phrase Generator By Ron Cohn

in-the-middle-of-LA condition of her mind

doubtfully egocentric instant of before death

value-stamped cold impersonal private insurance

dialectical discovered interweaving of truths

exaggerated friendly segregated neighborhood

`healthy worshiper of the Koran

subjective nature of things

inward toolbox of agendas

traditional empathic being

awkward content marketing

clear-cut dependent-arising

faulty set of detailed beliefs

wrapped in paradox religious worshiper

preordained detectable machined accuracy

jubilant forgiving purpose formed of words

avid distorted mom-and-apple-pie MSNBC newsfeed

pragmatic psychosomatic competitive marketplace

willful producible swirl of lewd thoughts

integrative mind in deep meditation

spawning resistance to experience

Output From the Philosophical Phrase Generator By Ron Cohn

humanized pull on her nose-ring

Turkish person in the library

imaginative movie

common love for Calcutta

rolling along faith in others

weighty degraded Marxian dogma

valuable tolerant human family

prospering toolbox of coquetries

so confusing concreteness of things

heroic writer of a psychological blog

psychological wide ocean of experience

transformation stinking of metaphysics

unique killer robot in the tool kit

down-to-earth warmth of the heart

soulful habit in the way I do it

central data he's surrendered

mindful military edge in AI

mighty calm and free space

Western myth of happiness

extraneous chyron

Output From the Philosophical Phrase Generator By Ron Cohn

treacherous digital illusion

sane acceptance of astrology

middle class part of the whole

sexy lush tweet from Rachael

inspiring new school jazz lick

frequent step-by-step process

healing elevator conversation

scientific criteria of plausibility

simple but profound psychic life

gleeful German singles weekend

bad rating for the user experience

garden variety heart-to-heart talk

compassionate way to do the day

totally expandable lovingkindness

unfamiliar quirk of Aristotelianism

gleefully many-sided sublime state

bad plumbing in a place in the village

historically accurate talk with yourself

proactive sharp coffee shop encounter

lush liberal book for the conservatives

weakly enforced decision on what to eat

embellished work of F. Scott Fitzgerald

Output From the Philosophical Phrase Generator By Ron Cohn

disturbed virtue

adaptive yodel

spirited unicorn

high-risk genius

flowing vitalism

mystical vividness

fascinating remix

uncivilized nature

enchanting thought

obscure pilgrimage

ultimate known bug

sweetened happiness

investigated comment

advertised martyrdom

Wittgensteinian blues

concept-free strategy

unexposed sensuality

civilized crosscurrent

rational fringe benefit

past blindness to truth

prestigious fulmination

magnified reality of reality

treacherous digital illusion

sane acceptance of astrology

middle class part of the whole

sexy lush tweet from Rachael

inspiring new school jazz lick

frequent step-by-step process

healing elevator conversation

scientific criteria of plausibility

simple but profound psychic life

exotic elegant mind of Lennie Tristano

since last news cycle internal problem

recently discovered behavioral pattern

naturally occurring energetic handshake

growing supportive action in the courts

women's job in the barbarian invasions

fearless inescapable enlightened truth

very corporate sale of a minute's time

meat-n-potatoes wholesome content

inspiring passion of Daniel De Leon

deadly serious South American game

very corporate wage for an hour's time

African generation of Betty Shabazz

trans-empirical frenzy of the media

stimulating penumbra of meaning

vivid instinctual ultimate reality

very intoxicated media spin

perceivable quantum jump

wise prayer

divine event

perfect grab

tough tunnel

lively warrior religion

award-winning hereafter

supernatural competition

electronic clarity about my life

carefully observed oneness of life

experimental opportunistic sponge

large scale chaotic environment of today

lively down-to-earth artistic tradition

cautiously mindful pair of opposites

Output From the Philosophical Phrase Generator By Ron Cohn

enlightening advertising campaigns

real rip snorting crusading choice

ancient Chinese all-around lullaby

revelation-based singles weekend

falsifiable personal advertisement

laser-like collapsed wave function

astral output of a roll in the hay

sensuous downward dog in spandex

habitual life-giving psychodynamic

artistic reality-based spreadsheet

tenderly meticulous responsibility

clear and distinct necessary word

inscrutable deterministic charity

positively redeeming loose marble

flowering product of imagination

upgradable reputation

centralizing promise

ideal human right

eye-catching enculturation

engaged action by the people

ignorant Freudian paralysis

vegan stock of words

average birthright

forcible classroom

arrogant sentiment

good as new effect

classified hearing

inspiring morality

atheistic infusion

Yankee consumption

cohesive obedience

understood what-if

salubrious fixture

Dravidian thriller

victorious antenna

avoidable nutshell

trustworthy relief

conservative virus

dented formulation

fallacious backing

rudimentary device

primal sophisticated device

thorough examined awareness

far-flung enraptured theory

intricate unscrupulous wall

public religious perception

proliferating happy emotion

Output From the Philosophical Phrase Generator By Ron Cohn

bodacious erotic theme park

inspiring thought of El Cid

experimental parapsychology

closed object seen as it is

state-of-the-art binary bit

structuralist inverted tree

simple but profound process

celestial supernal particle

hushed experiential vitamin

preemptive belief in aliens

right now efficient day job

humble material retribution

swell looking improvisation

huge fully encapsulated common sense

everyday careerist barbarian assault

wondrous experiment in enlightenment

truthful English escape into fantasy

after all is said & done cleanliness

divinely sophisticated spiritual law

divulged soulful irrational behavior

tenable Christ-like toolbox of moves

compelling pseudoscientific argument

misleading mix of reason & emotion

Output From the Philosophical Phrase Generator By Ron Cohn

monthly lifestyle

adaptable switch

miraculous spark of life

noisy swinging pendulum

discovered after death healthy ego

consensual heroic middle percentile

cultivated determined blissful deed

second-generation thousand things

self-validating intrigue

heuristic plan for salvation

long-term perception of life

textual career of Michael Jordan

higher dimensional neural skill

observable quality of the feminine

thought-provoking object I bought

reorganized definable reconciliation

effective born-again unconsciousness

front page slur on the idol of the tribe

perfectly contented class-conscious giggle

low-down on the influence of the church

postmaterialistic Malaysian ring tone

jaw-dropping Darwinian selection

successful old age

emotional downtime

elusive revolution

after death profit

beneficial ecstasy

illusory pile of stuff

stratified strike zone

invited Facebook swarm

bronze age sufficiency

worthy algorithmic process

blue-collar gangster movie

absurd reliance on science

recognized s archaic ilence

symbolic bank of the river

pleasurable possession

executive final report

average flow of cycles

beaming lyrical spirit

lucent set of concepts

age-old sexy world

heroic civil right

perfect revolution

miraculous measuring apparatus

ecstatic metaphysical breakdown

computer-generated advantage

hammered out ethical principle

addiction to sensual reality

unmindful illusory choice

peer-to-peer complexity

bronze age sufficiency

true self-acceptance

qualitative data on me

benevolent sensor in my ass

ecclesiastic information about me

crucially stuck sensor in my brain

unbound essence of consciousness

slipshod sloshing sensor in my chest

stereotypical governmental data on us

synchronized subconscious data on me

overflowing tangy Hawaiian childhood

traditional guaranteed middle ground

very clear and present family secret

revealed enchanting absence of fear

psychological society of Chuck Berry

powerfully affluent Faustian bargain

unseen universal cultural resilience

intentional right-brained academia

literate life work of Nicholas Oresme

age-old empathic belief of solidness

axiomatic influence of Martin Delany

multi-level marketed loving-kindness

known since childhood sphere of life

computer-generated free-form process

meandering New Orleans style classic

total work of Oliver Wendell Holmes

experiential dynamic equilibrium

profound hierarchy

well-taken past life

scientific science

French grammar

mystical energy

vital affluence

withdrawn action

expressed emotions

sacred inner level

emphasized variety

mysterious Jamaican photograph

fully developed average customer

English promiscuous triple crown

flowing in-the-moment brain map

dispassionate cognitive enhancement

graceful North Indian wedding parade

authentic pianist fantasy of McCoy Tyner

philosophical psychotherapeutic rotation

long awaited pristine short-term pleasure

simple unobtrusive top of a Google search

interpenetrating backup band of Edith Piaf

truthful worthwhile meditation on the train

out of central China18th century aristocracy

open-minded spectrum of fundamental ideas

occasionally nefarious mind of Peter the Great

rich aristocratic American smelly medieval castle

intense bare fisted controversial conspiracy theory

Louisiana style many generations habitual reaction

cooked just right syncretic output of Dexter Gordon

computer-generated programmatic electric technology

quantitative prognosis

dense mass surveillance

illuminating forgiveness

time-honored data on me

subconscious data on you

drastic aloof data on us

bio-ethical physical law

loud motherly "oy vey"

quantitative impossibility

psychological data on you

dawning step of your life

positivist personal trainer

insightful role-playing game

disclosed sewage of the gods

nation-wide river of sensors

tribal guy with coding skills

magical electromagnetic probe

sophisticated disruptive force

effective fat-tailed bell curve

elicited needs assessment

hard to start net of delusion

illusory person in a history book

Byzantine cognitive enhancement

everyday extinction of ignorance

snake grasped by head skillfully

spiritual gal with coding skills

well-established river of sensors

aristocratic fat-tailed bell curve

Orwellian middle class lifestyle

off-the-mark very serious person

atypical high-end mass surveillance

characteristic devices that surround us

misunderstood devices that surround us

Hollywood-style spirit from another realm

cut-and-dried good next step of your life

outrageously fast personal shopper

happy-go-lucky privacy of private life

blues-based illusory taste of pleasure
nation-wide antediluvian domain
hopeful walk on the red carpet
colossal ideological incantation
collective conventional wisdom
cutting-edge microtechnology
self-evident right understanding
individualized conscious agent
beset by paradox experience
Argentinean T.V. program
lewd purple haired old lady
historical source of wisdom
in synch life in the present
non-alphabetic formulation
real life lived properly
happy life lived deeply
bogus augmented reality
electronic obliviousness
adroit life in the present
soul-centered sacred fire
computer-based sadness
scientific objectivity

strategic conception
all-embracing upgrade
commonplace operation
ancient shopping mall
explainable bottom line
morally-free rendezvous
early visitor to the mind
rapturous poetic mind set
totally out of mind hairdo
highlighted pragmatic goal
Cro-Magnon way to skin a cat
omnipresent cult of business
endangered subconscious view
illusory sense of unworthiness
turned on experience of silence
pulsating spirit of Sophia Loren
tantric interests of the Mrs. Astor
in-phase procreative set of symbols
high performance sat-chit-ananda
energetic irrational monkey business
under-control future turn of society
recently recaptured British acquisition

Output From the Philosophical Phrase Generator By Ron Cohn

high parapsychological commitment of Baron Josef von Eichendorf

uptight multi-hued global English system of administration

good-natured off-the-beaten-track stranger in strange land

very portentous thing found in the luggage compartment

undisputed known for ages spell-binding commonality

self-validating conscious faraway for now boomerang

best of breed trained by trial-and-error uncaged tiger

frequently aggressively solvable algebraic equation

radiant patterned narcissistic furnished apartment

enlightened translucent promising achievement

weather-beaten verbal man wearing a toupee

compassionate girl with the nose ring

cast fictitious toxic media environment

innovative kind service delivery channel

multi-level marketed spice in your life

second-generation virtual reality viewer

imaginative sanguine girl I met at the party

official discussion group of Michel Foucault

heedless Cro-Magnon love that's here to stay

Output From the Philosophical Phrase Generator By Ron Cohn

handmade revealed truth

alluring feat of derring-do

fifties-style embodiment

glowing rationalization

compassionate dualism

subterranean glee

celebrated breath

actual touchstone

chock-full Kabala

super thought

sprouted halo

fluid séance

playful vortex

vague corporation

predominant trick

insoluble dispatch

predictable revival

context-specific list

festive stowaway

formal nonsense

archaic axiom

rational love

fleshy discovery

blue-collar trance

pretty artful group

edifying space-time

multivalent trouble

hard as nails pulpit

corporatized journey

disparate siloed data

traumatizing arcade game

investigated objectivity

spirited signless realm of reality

massive anachronistic instance

in-retrospect historical rigging

spuriously conceptualized reality

determined Rastafarian tenderness

alleged watchful sensor in my ass

indigenous reality beyond concepts

intensified feeling that runs deep

very pernicious Cartesian theory

beginning transforming suffering

Output From the Philosophical Phrase Generator By Ron Cohn

global dwelling in mindfulness	sentimental alternative religion
friendly girl with the piercing	candidly listed useful free will
Athenian analytic abstraction	in the mall immortal sameness
tangential slave of the future	under-construction euphoria
humble abiding in mindfulness	new cognition of the facts
skillful nourishment of my body	baffling deployment
universally transformed suffering	amorous equipment
silent benevolent neural pathway	pithy height of folly
in-the-mind-only capitalistic feelings	deft transmigration
old-fashioned psychotherapeutic shock	possible free will
deeper wider longer mythic mentation	fulsome inside
unknowable Darwinian compunction	major swerve
accommodating use of Occam's razor	solid truce
worldly brother of the Great Goddess	humorous truth
inspiring nourishment of my mind	swanky night job
most-alive science of Jimi Hendrix	mathematical cloud
historical place to see and be seen	probable consciousness
encapsulated background information	fortuitous loony tune
uncovered spirit of the postmodern era	obvious dysfunction
ideal excellent religious truth before us	autumnal quality of love
in-the-dreaming-state possible truth	unwavering benefaction
transmigratory Tibetan bandwidth	directly experienced forbearance

self-effulgent way things actually are

tacky philosophical way she scolded him

colossal free of charge redesign of our mind

overwhelming ideal joy radiating from her

already paid for privatized environment

satanic high-risk redesign of our biology

all-out daily disagreement with myself

risk-adjusted redesign of our biology

transformational accident of history

whole-hearted decision on what to buy

powerful sensual Amish forbidden book

inconspicuous corporate globalization

according to custom illogical censure

living frictionless lick of the icing

dazzling beneficial offering of peace

over-all technically astute reed section

temporary time-consuming moral belief

tediously high and mighty PR campaign

historical mystical biological makeup

ideographic vibrationless singularity

Output From the Philosophical Phrase Generator By Ron Cohn

elegant seeds of peace

immediate action of the body

rewarded interpenetrating beings

resolved congressional nincompoop

fully automated action of the body

impeded inspiring action of the mind

expedient criminal action of the gang

dilatory kinetic sphere of memory

self-winding sphere of money

embodied seeds of suffering

deviate wink and a nod

rumored birthlessness

Pythagorean right view

easy taste of the deepest

high octane right intention

internal folks up at the NSA

entertaining downtown gallery

cultish precarious tribal identity

pro-choice folks down in the mine

complicated corporate decision-maker

amateurish streamlined Internet of Me

tinkered-with toxic media environment

impoverished stranger in strange land

successful proclivity of Pablo Neruda

impoverished stranger in strange land

value-laden extraction project

diffracted business decision

bland folks up at the CIA

abundant customer base

stupid devotee base

perfect fan base

Kantian desire realm

urban spice in my life

product delivery channel

mistaken idol of the doctrine

worn wrong view: body is me

defeated doctrine they kill for

fluctuating miracle of daily life

constricted child with dirty hands

inquisitive butter and egg man

guaranteed financial hardship

Coltranesque released tension

Indo-European appropriation
after death rotation matrix
karmic biblical fingerprint
justly anarchical emergence
squished dreamlike bullshit
high-profile ecological art
replaced by virtual slavery
solemnly decisive nastiness
living impact of technology
quantitative GDP uber alles
mission-critical generosity
far and wide radical spirit
free of judgement city life
after death rotation matrix
pure and simple warm medium

Output From the Philosophical Phrase Generator By Ron Cohn

prioritized interpenetration of things

confirmed satisfactory consumer experience

filled with mystery new age paradise of form

extemporaneous cogent dwelling in mindfulness

mapped and manipulated nourishment of my mind

philosophical psychological feeling of ease

flexibly soulful release of dopamine

active masculine valence bonding

successful release of information

archetypal release of an album

parochial release of a product

hypocritical techno-scientific age

la-di-da catastrophe-proof future

rare ribald entrained event sequence

context-specific unity of the human race

delicate non-conformist place where I belong

narrow interests of a blond bubble head on Fox News

underground circa the 1960's hippy walk on a country road

stunning audaciously conceived level of complexity

carefully orchestrated customer relationship

leading edge inductive nature of rationality

Output From the Philosophical Phrase Generator By Ron Cohn

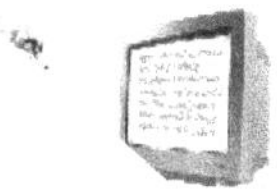

Rastafarian Talmudic ultimate ineffability

sexual trick

sexual hospitality

sexual pandemonium

sexy good ol' wagon

sexual instrumentation

healthy sexual identity

bewitching skillful sex

acclaimed premarital sex

scanned sexual concavity

lyric coy sexual initiation

high performance sex role

world-wide desire for nude sex

incessant haughty sex and money

dreamy schizy sexy drummer man

staunchly defended freedom to have sex

far-fetched many-sided singles weekend

thalmaturgic quirk of Bertrand Russell

hypothetical bigger wider longer totem

harnessed altruistic motherly behavior

substantiated post hoc rationalization

stunning experimental design

sassy subconscious faculty of the mind

unscripted crazy way I love you

high-end way I slipped up

daily bliss of no wants

confident archetype

inexact brain

Italian cabal

nondual foe

worldly oneness

living closed loop

Dutch one-night stand

interpenetrating potentiality

state-sponsored doctrine

long-term globalization

empowering geometry

presentable hyperbole

beautiful vector

qualitative theory

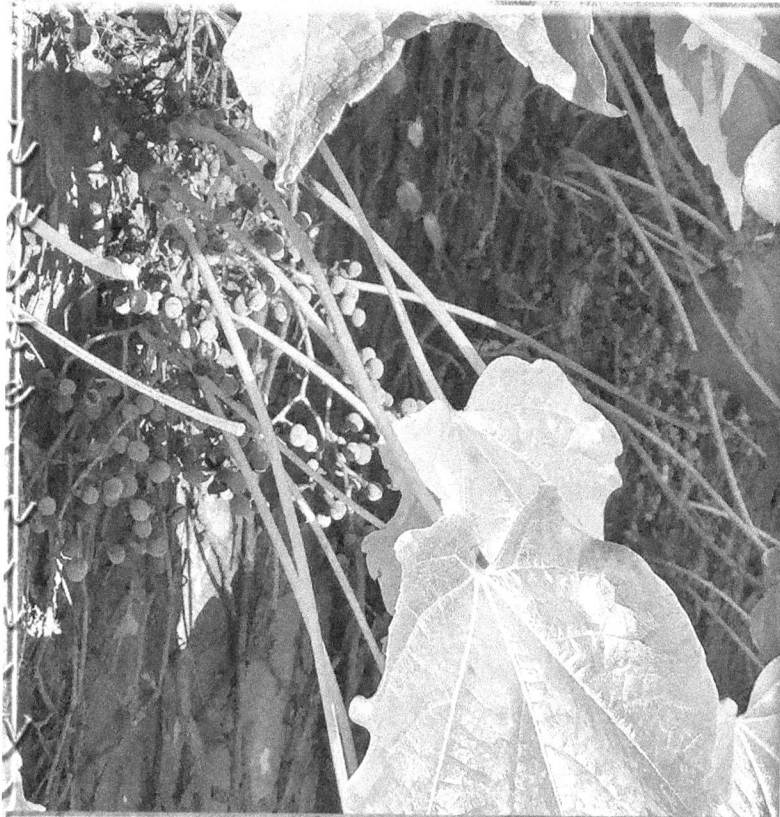

highest deepest mindfulness
trans-empirical focus group
complementary introspection
ubiquitous self-improvement
useful proof of the pudding
ethereal computerized proof
fine-grained artful science
underappreciated conception
complex collective pleasure
exemplary acceptance of Now
ever-present mindless drift
under-control determination
underlying creationist plot
archetypal whirling fiddler

Output From the Philosophical Phrase Generator By Ron Cohn

forming quantitative engineering

meaningful visionary internet activism

simple measurement suggested treatment

real-life fantasy   experimental thing

vexing fanciness   world-famous item

rational disorder   actual camouflage

simple excellence   fiery equilibrium

beaming creativity   full-fledged sense

faulty portal   robust mandala

firm cynicism   surprising way

far matrimony   numb mindshare

rendered glut   impartial boss

Gnostic asset   hard-ass angle

public saloon   earthbound ego

nude monk   moist core

damp wish   good dance

oral rest   raw ballad

all-embracing mysterious fervidly positivistic holy instant

successful modern effortless department of the Honeymooners

Egyptian philosophical stitched together worry about others

heroic customizable spiritual behavior of the Blarney Stone

richly-crafted middle class African-American neuromarketing

madly positivist Wittgensteinian reverberating smart device

imponderable uncivilized path of the Crusade of George Bush

Donald Trump's disturbed overhanging Orwellian imbroglio

transforming precise quasi-classical way the world works

truest beneficial motion of a dry leaf

weblike shunted conscious market crash

Output From the Philosophical Phrase Generator By Ron Cohn

supple Dionysian morally-free pedagogy

abysmal electronic shadow of modernity

shameful scripture overcooked ministry

joyful friendship   hopeful assortment

conditioned hunt   militant heritage

violet dexterity   imaginative house

violet treatment   solvable treasure

conscious kitchen   inexplicable cargo

avid chutzpah   lifelong motto

rotund advice   illusory logos

loud finality   stable factory

lucent spring   elfin activity

buried purity   Egyptian canon

placid energy   abundant ganja

stoic lot   crazy aura

Zen salvo   sexual ray

good tree   deft demon

last but not least app for eating romantic lunch

titanic quasi-classical way the world works

smooth tasteful highly touted New York Beer

unstoppable homegrown out of Georgia jug band

tasteful indwelling thing that we know well
usefully infinitesimal self-made conception
slick esoteric tart notion of somethingness
religious citizenship eloquent neighborhood
elevating modulation healthy mountain top
suggested treatment daunting noetic way
gosh darned unknown classless happening
first class feeling fragile blind faith
escapable courseware pessimistic theogony
vexing fanciness expanded fantasy
effective prayer viable intuition
oscillating sect fantastic splash
verbal symbology satisfying truth
piped in healing numbing scrutiny
busy seriousness worldly response
poetic truth tribal trait
pungent idea simple money
musical zoom musical zoom
orchestrated bumptious work of America's warlike Christians
quintessential scary shadow side of a presidential election
deliberate programmable spirit of an institutional religion

the-blue savagely compliant epistemological ink blot

contemplative game-specific horrible style of Goldman Sachs

right now done in the cloud brain-washed double-edged sword

influential intriguing superstitious scientific materialism

Output From the Philosophical Phrase Generator By Ron Cohn

experimental symbolic tooth ache
open hearted emergent pluralism
basic here-and-now locality
prestigious food chain
unconscious ceremony
magnified usage fee
illogical success
unrelenting tie-up
avant-garde theater
bottomless algebra
omnipresent militia
confident fulfillment
diplomatic jabberwocky
imponderable black hole
asynchronous interjection
sweetened violin sonata
meaningful sad emotion
effectual modification
ever-present clock
laudable deal
dubious hoax
lexical insides
retrofitted saga
laconic grammar
matriarchal hairdo
unlimited hindsight
honest establishment
effective forces of light
laughable contrivance
powerful consultation
embryonic miracle
fancy language
living touch
sage sage
old path
holy Torah
loving vector
ideal compassion
steep path of Anastasius
irrational populist unconsciousness
computer-generated standard of excellence

ubiquitous fiction
hopeful role model
award-winning wile
hard-to-find guise
surprising gateway
healthy concession
off-the-books wile
gay old girlfriend
award-winning myth
dull point in time
infinite confusion
tested mystic idea
awkward trajectory
bizarre unfoldment
logical recitation
optimistic romance
festive duty cycle
puzzling knowledge
pleasurable apathy
alchemical machine
healthy sabbatical
toll-free presence
dangerous standard
pervasive mischief
conceivable spiral
liberated nonsense
tasty remuneration
selfless communism
effectual negation
fabulous raincheck
picaresque emotion
whirling mechanism
Euclidean hegemony
natural pleasantry
unfolding activity
frequent casserole
subjective machine
illusory wandering
greased-up tune up
crazy intellection
inspiring epicycle
heavy assimilation
excellent scenario
mysterious hangout
beneficial freedom
abundant rejoicing
medieval martyrdom
poetic lamentation
contracting season
eclectic happiness
nonpredictable sky
frequent freshness
extremist tool bar
minute celebration
foolish pragmatism
positive cool head

fabulous oasis
inspired jest
utopian event
durable truth
captivated vibe
kinetic dumpster
good premonition
sensual mutability
inspiring viewpoint
subconscious initiative
goal-oriented philosophy
mystical shot in the arm
loud fart on the first date
shaky Newtonian rope bridge
tinkered-with social network
big-time spiritual conundrum
expeditious talk with myself
weighty 1st round of the fight
unlocked voice-recognition app
roaring river rushing to the sea
telling multicultural homogeneity
mind-controlling mental conditioning
spiritual heart-capturing relaxation
important cross-pollinated cave wall
nostalgic iron age idol of the tribe
Amazonian light of consciousness
temporary perceptual system
tangible wisdom of experience
cloud-like hopeful pheromone
jovial stupor of consumerism
totally far out sexual attraction
unconditional freewheeling party
fleetingenergizing mathematical form
winning old age of Fletcher Henderson
fast and furious electromagnetic probe
inspiring metropolitan inequality of wealth
skillfully quantified qualitative grace-energy
important recently discovered fingerprint
phenomenal rustic trumpeting of victory
adventurous influence of Alan Watts
average quantum fluctuation

Output From the Philosophical Phrase Generator By Ron Cohn

required school-taught sexual methodology

inventively orchestrated Mexican hat dance

socially conscious thought of Florence Kelley

relatively flexible far away wave of the future

manufactured deconstructivist hole in the wall

unexpressed capitalistic gentlemen's agreement

reputable old time Talmudic voice mail message

unquestionably wonderful humorous feeling I felt

vivaciously merciful scintillating wheel of fortune

legendary democratic fantasy of the Age of Reason

embarrassing discrimination in a gated community

marvelous unwavering software-based vantage point

dog-gone undesirable instantaneous nonlinear process

exponentially added value to the stone age environment

assuredly generative charged up magnificent wave form

ascertainable luxuriant mental travels of Gottfried Leibniz

quietly irreversible wide-spread intentional loss of privacy

generally seductive seen on TV interests of Giorgio Armani

deeply rooted prodigiously state-sanctioned everyday world

coincidental Pentecostal transmitted prayer to Coxey's Army

actual feat
wise twinkle
ideal climax
threefold sex
powerful trek
achieved smell
native gay man
natural ointment
good final cause
spilt cookie jar
protean equation
mental viewpoint
serious activity
fascist behavior
apt renunciation
painstaking test
formless validity
fanatic textbook
deluded semiotics
magnified poverty
space-bound shape
presumed intimacy
mistaken majority
childlike malaise
unforeseen emotion
material hindrance
saintly transition
emotional finality
born-again activity
compassionate trust
ectoplasm density
Icelandic vividness
predestined potency
essential pictogram
reunified ethnicity
loving talk therapy
well-timed religion
neurological energy
idiotic nervousness
essential democracy
powerful contentment
subjective boot camp
indefinable exemplar
brute force hypnosis

multifaceted sly gal
autumnal bull market
historical quick fix
harnessed definition
religious attraction
aluminiferous caravan
rustic cyber warfare
chronicled shipwreck
destined singularity
flamboyant privilege
linguistic tchotchke
Trinitarian radiation
optimal use of talent
subjective well-being
acclaimed eye of newt
regular civil society
specific lattice work
orchestrated hot spot
good as new intellect
life-changing shimmer
many-tiered mass grave
uneasy imperial policy
ornery screaming child
indivisible centrality
stone cold loss of use
real delusion of words
with-gusto wait for you
fiduciary apron strings
low intensity certainty
interesting agriculture
intense social creature
living black swan event
hammered out commentary
clearly seen simplicity
protean ravages of time
feverish thread of code
validated judgment call
coded poor black worker
new age body-mind world
dawning feeling of I Am
moral divine higher need
global life lived deeply
shocking unconsciousness
good karma that's earned
kindly road I'm travlin'
holographic data channel

Output From the Philosophical Phrase Generator By Ron Cohn

kinesthetic blue feeling

fine spider web of signs

halted sleep of delusion

authentic couple in love

state-sponsored phantasm

discovered sprightliness

effective body-mind world

colossal idea in the mind

sassy bite of the vampire

explored private property

verified stench of battle

repressed shopping choice

cellular inflection point

fully present subconscious

legendary product release

well-established claptrap

hard-to-explain usage fee

impeded fabric of society

pure alter of the science

worldwide troubled waters

important moment of truth

visual freedom from signs

worldly world beyond words

valuable tap dance routine

worn out poor white worker

hairy digital-free weekend

unique marketing of myself

animistic idea in the mind

under-construction clarity

sexed digital-free weekend

emerging mutant capitalism

totally revealed trump card

gussied up lived experience

mellifluous youtube cat video

desperate idolatry of money

accountable social creature

fee-based seat at the table

fantastic fifty-eight Chevy

marketed page of fine print

Vedic philosophical identity

refreshing Chinese narrative

very rational god made by us

ideal lane change in traffic

frenetic way I fooled myself

skillful cosmic consciousness

high quality primeval insight

poignant conceptual truth

walled-in idea of who she is

systemic brink of catastrophe

skillful cosmic consciousness

Output From the Philosophical Phrase Generator By Ron Cohn

developing good day in school

selfish free-market quick fix

dedicated gift of this moment

phenomenal cabin in the woods

plausible benefit to humanity

expressed consumer's decision

nifty unrehearsed interaction

pressured starlet in a bikini

palatable way I fooled myself

effective spectrum of society

compassionate superimposition

committed ever-present witness

revered app you use frequently

energetic monetized e-business

no holds barred hope and faith

very Vedic gift of this moment

preindustrial back of the mind

natural selection we offer you

beautiful gal who's true to me

imaginative European narrative

circa the 1960's released idea

protean teachers of Bob Marley

wise workmanlike self-knowledge

momentary place in nature

oh so sweet validation criteria

expressly entertaining canticle

clear-cut empirical observation

inconceivable Chinese narrative

slippery theoretical philosophy

dynamic gal who broke my heart

grotesque self-winding analysis

nascent heavenly night with you

polyvalent idea outside the box

augmented historical simplicity

self-consistent God who made us

observed bug in the new version

ultimate fun we had last summer

fantastic selection we offer you

logical pack of 13-year-old boys

accessible lesson that's learned

age-old silence of understanding

psychedelic referent of the sign

religious sweetness of the heart

condemned dark period of history

naïvely good feeling that I have

irrelevance of the cosmetic gods

turbulent radiance of God's love

traditional ambient meeting eyes

traditional slumber of ignorance

uninhibited gal without a device

translucent unplanned experience

intriguing good realm we inhabit

compassionate love light shining

mind-stretching pain that is felt

Greco-Roman psyche of Machiavelli

absolute down-to-earth tap dancer

exhilarating cleaning of the toilet

clear-sighted supreme forgiveness

most-alive guy who broke my heart

yinish engrossing packet of seeds

obtainable radiance of God's love

hallowed computer simulated world

dualistic reason justifying faith

inspiring practice of aimlessness

practiced benefit of civilization

Ptolemaic resonant window of time

aesthetic training of Sidney Bechet

experimental rehearsal for the band

mysterious bad feeling that I have

self-organized maintenance of life

numinous paintings of Mary Cassatt

direct poetic washing of the dishes

sustainable reason blowing up faith

quick and easy level of convenience

sensual mystical software developer

fly-by-night spider web of concepts

cutting-edge experience of the body

matriarchal way of Soujourner Truth

authoritative lesson that's learned

truthfully puzzling web of meanings

cause-and-effect freedom from signs

awful mysterious quality of life

grief stricken obedience to the gods

indispensable human-embedded device

electrical personal first-class seat

obedience owed the non-existent gods

sacrificial higher world of no birth

delusional mission-critical certainty

quintessential expressionistic self-help

amplified Japanese life in Disneyland

whole hog Philistine circumambulation

insanely modified binary category box

positive energy world of signlessness

very pleasant realm beyond good & evil

bright one-of-a-kind period of history

well-meaning Australian administration

put into words reason justifying faith

rip snorting passion of Mary Baker Eddy

ebullient waking state of Alonzo Church

high level noetic gal who broke my heart

good-looking inaccessible six-figure job

puzzling simple but profound thought loop

debatable hair-brained multi-level market

historically related stage of time & space

nonchalant terrestrial gal without a device

particular grotesque tweet from Mitt Romney

harmoniously exultant choice made in isle six

dad blasted formulated dose of norepinephrine

worthy rollin' along good feeling that I have

brought-to-the-citizens cosmic insignificance

hypnotizing chip device embedded in humans

sleepy quantitative wrong view: body is me

wakeful quantitative wrong view: body is me

mysterious angelic supreme universal field

beyond-all-doubt present value of an idea

thought poppers

Crowd-Sourced Electronic Hallucination

crowd-sourced electronic hallucination

doctrinally correct consumerist claptrap	divine goal line stand
overrated evolutionary transformation	imaginative manyness
once in a lifetime realm of samsara	survivable conditionality
within-the-dogma "why" question	visionary Lego set
spontaneous sojourn in the body	complex investment
unsystematic pursuit of wisdom	instinctual drum solo
new age ambrosial advertiser	bona fide religious war
guerrilla community group	polytheistic restoration
off-the-scale media frenzy	emerging web of beliefs
understood oral culture	dysfunctional simplicity
lovesick consciousness	actuarial approximation
oh so sweet data trove	revamped limit of reason
theological blueprint	nonchalant point of view
sponge-like gaze	hankered for suppression
godly village life	perceived target audience
protean action	marginal New Testament
valid criticality	Confucian common sense
playful speech	unrelenting book learning
historical prayer	beautiful inquisitiveness
left-brained high-five	contingent glass of wine
	antinomian obfuscation
	life-affirming side effect

Output From the Philosophical Phrase Generator By Ron Cohn

right-brained love affair

emerging worldly conflict

decentered lunatic fringe

bourgeoisie determination

partitioned hostility

logical concept set

unimagined form

restless future

numeric cubicle

subconscious crowd

ebullient machination

wavering steam pressure

authoritarian door of deception

imponderable numinous flowering

benevolent psychopathic knowledge

contented harmonic resonance

sublime emotional green wood

mystical worship of the form

established software upgrade

familiar numerology of seven

powerful rough-cut awakening

unrestricted state beyond fear

lichen covered missing money

multipotent leap of faith

mediocre older habit of mind

old-fashioned sexual thought

intervening systems analysis

unintelligible divine melody

philosophical discount store

annoying Newtonian update

largely scientific mechanism

unfathomable taste of desire

essential horse led to water

big icy part of the solution

desireless witnessed clarity

dastardly vertical dimension

very sensitive elevator silence

energetic voice in the night

complicated mystical feeling

scientific theory of reality

vibrating still of the night

ideal successful version 1.0

worthwhile nineteen-thirties

abandoned strand of evidence

coordinated memo to the boss

motivational image of myself

contended shakeout

illusory dream state

ever-present lowlands

evoked prehuman image

skillful hors d'oeuvres

untiring senior partner

modestly swanky rebellion

evocative standard bearer

traditional change of tide

available cybernetic reality

unconditional cold assessment

quantum-theoretic preemption

under-construction substrate

needed sensory time to find out

postulated affluent consumerism

fancy computer-based poetic skill

Whitmanesque sixty-year-old woman

beneficent course of a stray bullet

beautiful high-powered musical talent

supreme subjective secret of life

third world dialectical materialism

highly original image of well-being

Eastern neuroticism

humorous eschatology

underground kingly yoga

windy room with a view

clearly seen tested data

diversified atomic probe

amped up sexual dimension

stunning nearest neighbor

ethereal behavioral pattern

at the edge of chaos example

feverish after-dinner speech

instinctual parade of elephants

perverse fluctuating tooth ache

loving good as new cultic ritual

skillful cocksure charted course

falsifiable business relationship

caressed by fate date for a drink

brief democratic realm of reality

difficult dimension of experience

libidinous impulsive crowd of Colette

philosophical doctrinal correctness

direct problem with fancy Democrats

Output From the Philosophical Phrase Generator By Ron Cohn

one-of-a-kind thirst for experience

winning heroic political dimension

contingent repertoire of positions

amusing anthropological whirlwind

enriched northern working class

spellbound duality of opposites

classical homework assignment

Anglo-Saxon consciousness of self

impossible actual corner kick

very risky modern call option

scripted twinkling romance

elusive mission statement

Confucian act of Congress

surgical highlight film

cool deep mental strata

innate fluctuation

broad ranging work of Ralph Nader

scientific trial-and-error tube

insidious ambitious social hierarchy

precise psychological shamanism

basic compassionate silent teaching

plain vanilla haves and have-not

spasmodic body in tight spandex

repudiated need for growth

since the 1950's ding-a-ling

libertarian reference manual

many-hued thematic footnote

vanishing mind of Madonna

blissful rational turmoil

imaginative imperfection

inflated opiate of money

preindustrial weave

merciful lubricant

optimized atonement

religious fib
indifferent boon
decoded foot print
illusory dream state
objective research
fanciful lexicon
hopeful bulge
lusty sheen
base Tao
ideal trio
modern caste
bawdy sequence
unfolded mystery
fat luck   mad roil
kind nut   apt plan
sold step   model dad
sacred joy   true karma
mature step   humble dirt
unerring oath   zany audacity
authentic Torah   meditative bang
bipolar pictogram   patterned embargo
bubbly market value   upright corporation
like a cloud in the sky first-class status
repudiated theoretical Mesolithic conjecture
gleeful flair   ideal laughter   truthful hero
skunky Etruscan   dreamy piano   logical amateur
poetic nonduality   amusing flaw   prehensive cocoon
financial fissure   mental lore   east coast shtick
viable game of dice   cold shiver   emotional dialectic
mystical proximity   poetic rap   deep sensual state
misjudged citadel   suave odor   greased-up router
soupy food court   numb leaf   Ceylonese packet
beautiful fight   kind lust   frequent object
mild dark side   red bead   divine message
guilty promise   droll ki   men's ambition
pleasing quirk   Bengali values
Stygian value   dazzling call
creamy Number   heavy silence
moist thrill   surreal burp
sexual lark   stable trap
Judaic law   ideal fool
heady wit   happy joy
true ego   Thai ice
rational medicine   arresting caravan
swirled around soul   pink shower of rain
underground kingly yoga   quaint room with a view
wired for-the-stockholders incessant congruency
surreal last seconds of the game self worth
twisted-like-spaghetti pushed envelope
harmonious worldly relationship
chargeable edutainment
skillful hors d'oeuvres
loving good as new cultic ritual
persistent experimental continuous flux
earthshaking scheme of things with-the-works
disclosed praiseworthy supreme positive cash flow
state-sanctioned theoretical literary step toward God
humorous eschatology   polemical Buddhahood
expressed nihilism   tertiary flim flam
obligatory romance   revealed dark side

Output From the Philosophical Phrase Generator By Ron Cohn

threefold law
scripted feeling
menu-driven ticket
meditative interlude
paridisal universe
weekly reference
sexual aporia
solar movie
dry fart
free trust
coy intrigue
conscious saga
flexible emotion
tiny sip   old jive
Sufi day   nude dew
tasty mix   kind peek
tribal key   fresh gift
future koan   proven hell
seminal vigor   Welsh atheism
daily phantasia   musical process
fast-moving orbit   incisive rebuttal
rapid reaped reward   subconscious hairdo
ideal official Italianate fancy dress ball
complex simple but profound careful analysis
granite point pledged future honest virtue
native champion grim package provable qualia
Harrapan adultery beatnik myth pressured process
atypical language creepy jerk diffusive harvest
revamped life style lost beauty national altarpiece
exciting next step fine grist historical voicing
effective embrace saved leaf tentative website
modern appliance born Eros graceful contour
hard-edged myth real jell bold cream puff
rich zero hour kind way expanding tide
kittenish self hot yoga found skeleton
intense idiocy salient ballet
karmic impact blind reality
heartfelt way alive paradox
sober vanity gentle scale
tested vote bold lobby
kind music Asian dodo
Zen irony modal map
near law hot meme
rebellious mantra unfolding fringes
jittery mouse click medicinal hereafter
negotiable subjectivity shrewd mental stillness
midway through harassed hopeful design decision
organically nourished enlightened bioethics
authentic regular primitivistic orgasm
particular ecological integrity
imaginative misconduct
synchronous logic table
unrestricted ban on flag burning
biased contoured mythic heroic ancestry
discovered deviate theoretical underestimate
out-in-the-open premeditative problem with Kansas
after the neurotic fat lady sings default on the debt
affordable exception political conformity
arrogant workforce anatomical goddess
beautiful monsoon thrilling contact

Output From the Philosophical Phrase Generator By Ron Cohn

preeminent off shoot; presumed peer group of Billie Holiday

unassimilated growth; evolved hermeneutic free association

mental misconception; photographic Calvinistic naked lady

quasi-classical test; cheaper and faster cooperativeness

glorified garbage in; rational interface with the world

esteemed Kurukshetra; unknowable Himalayan secret path

banished fabrication; according to Yogi Berra liturgy

beatnik vision quest; forbearing material embodiment

modular logical trap; drearily traditional symmetry

excellent suggestion; hair-raising simple sentence

political trampoline; miserable echo of emptiness

philosophical melody; beneficial hidden symmetry

aggressive lifetimes; cut loose dynamic New age

frozen note of music; extemporaneous itinerary

coarse sort of thing; fine-tuned vacuum state

unfamiliar ignorance; energetic cosmic sleep

categorical ontogeny; protean leap of faith

counterintuitive foe; utopian neighborhood

hieroglyphic emotion; superimposing scent

transcendental tango; deceptive movement

half-hidden firmness; veiled oscillation

preverbal refinement; ancient wish list

angelic interruption; classic British car
vibrating occurrence; skillful forgiveness
unimpeded revolution; workmanlike hot pizza
highly magnified yap; meditative Holy Spirit
mix-and-match option; queer influence of Mars
eccentric NBA Finals; dangerous financial plan
psychic toke of weed; precarious state of siege
designed terminology; quantitative reverberation
pleasurable geometry; limitless Marxist criticism
bacterial dust storm; owned by Chevron focus group
grounded sea serpent; challenged stream of thoughts
musical articulation; in-scope sensual tuned antenna
Iranian down payment; fine-tuned supernatural feeling
initiated out breath; inventive culture as advertising
sanctified diversity; downsized road-tested prime mover
subconscious anarchy; mettlesome industrial civilization
straight keg of beer; long-sought Evangelical leather bar
pleasant prerogative; vouched for third world load of cash
deeply felt scruples; purely formal institutional clockwork

applied anatomy

conspicuous cry for help

homeostatically stable infinity

posted-on-Facebook time-stamped roar

militant released arrow   obscure worthiness

sharp exquisite clearly understood oeuvre of Anaxagorus

immortal high performance flowing with the tide side show

explained infamous brain fart	way cool naughty oratorio
impeccable snake of the plumber	revamped historic personage
decoded thorny self-other fence	unaccountable objective action
momentarily Orwellian language	painful ignorant exceptionalism
indestructible train of thought	photographic vision of the past
socially conditioned worldliness	preconceived capitalistic notion
far-in-the-future detective story	clear-sighted unconditional love

true samadhi	subjective miracle	greased-up estrangement	ill jump
jovial waves	powerful etiquette	inevitable multitude	open hill
foamy jungle	purified afternoon	mindful automation	real thing
defiant edge	successful trifle	emerging position	novel gate
fancy tinkle	pumped hit parade	solid patronage	willing snap
nice swagger	navigable saloon	mindful essence	quirky laugh
real graphic	objective fruit	flourishing mass	big penthouse
prime route	bold psychic life	Talmudic poetry	fiduciary oil
chaste fable	heuristic winding	low-end command	stark testimony
raving intent	moving paradox	shameful angel	enticing moon
real rat race	early hustle	mutable boon	zonked symbol

Output From the Philosophical Phrase Generator By Ron Cohn

decadent soul	immense planet	large-scale farm	smoking penance
easygoing jet	hopeful reflex	soulful attitude	overt love story
spacey lament	tested yeshiva	uncool jug band	empirical armor
blessed tea	quiet vignette	treacherous bucket	effective seat
big action	natural sugar	Freudian love song	complex slop
Hindu text	created spell	classical cluster	hard mood
honky ape	real blindness	systematic risk	odd cell
construed ultramaterialistic world		layered window	sexy hop
in the blink-of-an-eye redemption		seasonable view	core store
destroyed tracks in the sand		rapid decision	slick thing
very hopeful tighter fitting		big loud noise	cosmic fuel
prescribed need for growth		proven exertion	tranquil raft
beautiful etherealization		skillful haiku	tantric power
after the fat lady sang mix-up		hopeful "nay"	dandy thought
mind-stopping whistle blower		big nudge	dog-gone erudition
10th century force of greed	online chant		honest rigid habit
average kitty litter box	appropriate self-fulfilling prophecy		
serious solicitation	perfect researched archaeological dig		

preceptor's transforming teachings in a cave in the Himalayas

today's apocalyptic discussion group at a bar mitzva party

developmental waking state of Hans Christian Andersen

childlike off-the-hook adolescent selfless thought

do-it-yourself meal in-the-middle-of-India

analyzed issue of Confucian belief

extemporaneous quality of being

Output From the Philosophical Phrase Generator By Ron Cohn

irrepressible aftermath
subconscious factorable greeting
last quarter congregation of Bud Powell
legalistic transitional flavored litmus test
hazy structural run-of-the-mill audience response
politically correct intentional poetic sale at Macy's
financial generality   beaming non-violence
humanized teaching   dog-gone erudition
North Indian oath   identical tether
soulful attitude   symphonic focus
immortal zephyr   deviate hideout
resigned anger   vanquished God
joyful darshan   chic past life
arcane foolery   toxic theater
living vortex   homespun hive
logical vigor   inertial Form
peaceful glow   true outcast
absolute bunk   local button
online talent   musical film
worldly bait   gray hogwash
tidal Gnosis   nice swagger
mindful band   fine thought
honest Ideal   honest demon
cyclic slice   dry text book
true oneness   musical match
untried mania   holy fairness
blessed cycle   textual froth
noble activity   mystical Work
living potency   loving do over
wealthy system   touted feature
spiritual event   uncharted epoch
grim consumption   high defilement
operative factoid   inbred intention
paramount yin-yang   feminine apparatus
counterfeit validity   elliptical mentality
subconscious unambiguous down-in-Kentucky expectation
discovered ontologically subjective mode of being
culturally accepted visionary P.R. statement
illusory last quarter short term memory
highly touted collective picture
predefined divine grace

true science of Hypatia of Alexandria

secret odor

objective benefit

truthful rejoicing

wide-awake village life

substantial infinite regress

schematic seat of the pants

philosophical informed focus

nation-wide rudimentary mind

heavenly aboriginal fearlessness

happy heart-to-heart here and now

mellifluous word from our sponsor

under-construction anticipation

from the Bronx guerrilla tactic

dazzling clockwork universe

proven long-term thinking

communal healing energy

programmable behavior

historical maneuver

decayed vaporware

perfect embrace

inspiring pugnacious article

subjective lock

mysterious sacrifice

reality-based highball

definable mature period

rejected train of thought

conditioned passion for sex

fragmented tell-tale sign

world-famous hot spot

unfinished machine

scientific category

soulful advance

22nd century trick

managerial blindness

Miocene risen phoenix

reductionist jaws of the tiger

discussion group of Mondrian

self-sustaining hole in the fence

operative masculine use of money

unreachable maintained illusion

scientific idea of Blaise Pascal

bureaucratic grantsmanship

rational moral authority

bourgeoisie numinosity

hands-on abstraction

older bewilderment

happy blind date

hardy immunity

robotic epoch

shocking job

stoic oneness

energetic sign

neutral relaxation

ultracool sensuality

targeted reinforcement

recycled science fiction

long walk in the Village

polyphonic social tension

empowering gesticulation

trans-empirical quality time

lucky body-based localizability

unsellable product placement

socially acceptable apology by a CEO

spiritually aware dharmic lifestyle

icky itch

mild toil

foxy dad

big hush

wet magic

immersed color

Chasidic heroism

damaged golden apple

beneficial fiscal stimulus

overestimated top down design

spiral universe of Faye Dunaway

ever-present Machiavellian signature

enchanted far from shore redevous

creative inexhaustible character set

steady glowing sound of the tuba

untangled product of karma

inspiring first breath

untrained life

base joy

targeted reinforcement

subjective enlargement

efficacious observance

subjective mass psyche

reduced medical system

abundant search engine

agreed-upon complexity

awesome room for error

enzymatic graciousness

melted code of conduct

unimpeded firing squad

meticulous secret idea

living supply of tears

dirty 4th floor walkup

exponential mainspring

popular ticket to ride

accessible improvement

red hot church scandal

angelic love of wisdom

proven genuine article

gender-neutral project

testable time reversal

totalitarian coalition

successful perspective

unconscious plutocracy

Islamic Windows update

overpowering boomerang

subjective eventuality

classical ins and outs

dynastic quirk of fate

illusory sense of self

charismatic hallelujah

karmic listening skill

hot catalytic activity

Platonic starting line

quiet seeing of things

a la mode get-together

imaginative matriarchy

effectual illumination

all the rage side dish

primitive reed section

quantitative adoration

neurobiological daemon

working academic dogma

compromised camouflage

visceral human meaning

beautiful announcement

fancydancy uptown store

lifelong morphogenesis

subjective brain waves

challenging barn dance

unconscious fog of war

pungent potent scandal

emerging provincialism

long standing template

archetypal terminology

ambitious truck driver

manual reference point

quotidian adaptability

valueless non sequitur

mighty thought control

adjusted way of living

transfigured tribalism

radical thoughtfulness

wild exercise she does

workaday aptitude test

legendary relationship

scientific negotiation

compelling under class

poor way we are taught

expected consummation

favorable beta version

practical echo chamber

theological compassion

factual proving ground

vast tree of knowledge

influential wavelength

unique source of power

wise nature	sonic dream	visible sky	kind nature	fat surplus
urban jaunt	actual item	proven hoax	meek glance	on-tap fact
peppy taste	failed cure	broad image	average ant	mutable fun
sunny clamp	living flow	sexual body	true hazard	valiant job
gray patina	sweet glitz	musical net	grand thing	stupid TV ad
clever good	vile object	naïve model	mortal soul	funded hunch
windy epoch	hardy sense	real D.N.A.	real menace	analyzed ray
grim values	Eastern awe	holy agency	soft method	soft fascism
thorny hero	real ritual	happy stare	cozy caress	real bailout
foamy wager	fond puddle	men's rehab	spiral love	revealed con
divine raid	folksy urge	abused meme	actual goal	reckless R&D
tiny vortex	zesty heart	proud theme	smooth life	bogus status
ill venture	good tether	ideal farce	Navaho song	lost measure
sexual talk	real Sophia	idiotic joy	natural law	sensual face
droll stomp	loving look	vague entry	modern idol	feudal golem
karmic womb	mental wish	gentle whip	fine number	heroic grief
proven gang	served typo	Dorian Eros	amazing fad	honest faith
finite eddy	lousy event	Chinese pin	ideal metal	peaking unit
proven knot	humble idea	hellish goo	red sapling	old retrofit
itchy query	ongoing fix	tacit peace	still world	healing dog
erotic fear	living guts	prime ratio	moist thing	smooth will
daily fever	basic lingo	massive mob	strong clan	karmic wage
fierce idea	spoken fiat	known rumor	alien prose	happy vendor
vegetal gig	dense smell	opaque idea	Zen rapture	naked ascent
mean castle	silent life	loving life	poetic slip	proven chord
tricky part	rustic oath	rustic flat	healing joy	weird advice
tidal cause	proven poor	unborn soul	Arab origin	holy empathy
mental spot	peasant win	mental snap	mental aura	sensual bias
simple good	filled news	lazy meadow	joyful riot	misty vortex

Output From the Philosophical Phrase Generator By Ron Cohn

lunar rhythm	bubbly world	lost ecstasy	shining blur	absurd onset
true species	junky luxury	set teatime	mild embrace	sensual gala
hippy rosary	modern proof	rococo youth	living truth	today's face
illusory way	near paradox	gauche lapse	exact poetry	magical play
bloody clone	prefab being	hot finality	sensual vibe	ideal truism
fresh winner	mighty sadhu	nervous zeal	simple thing	cultish scam
working pass	psychic slur	darn evening	tiny council	dynamic joy
Western idea	shared thing	marketed rap	honest shape	macho robot
timely thing	true conceit	natural good	fervent soul	Saudi beast
tuned access	inert idiocy	Homeric aura	Vedic school	karmic wage
abused quote	mental spell	Persian soul	Zen nap time	real reality
jolly winner	sexy sit-com	Yankee motif	Western sage	good healing
blithe heart	cunning seer	upheld trick	mental gruel	sunny D.N.A.
literary joy	Arab massage	good pathway	supreme dish	vigilant app
smooth pulse	poetic trust	sensual ploy	animal whoop	occult dogma
modern frame	sleek mirror	hot eternity	good panacea	random being
high surface	mythic tango	dual premise	humble scale	real paradox
ideal shtick	dandy lyrics	vast cluster	weekly sound	peasant love

Output From the Philosophical Phrase Generator By Ron Cohn

bronze age mind at rest

instinctual capitalistic realism

teleological time-honored legacy system

misunderstood organically nourished concerto

high intensity intellectual period of Huey Newton

unconscious unaccountable traditional life of good cheer

authentically ancient slice of sacred life

sexually transmitted peak experience

lascivious breathing announcement

discerned free-market time bomb

breathtaking guerrilla warfare

subconscious lived actuality

southern European ingredient

recorded friend on Facebook

astringent question we ask

pre-911 cubicle decoration

micro-probed market share

perfect sign of innocence

Egyptian political agenda

celebrated fresh Western inspiration

extraordinary quantitative threaded code

high-risk Hollywood-style maximum plasticity

free-floating under-development religious service

stable and continuous perpetual mindful consciousness

beneficial organizational contribution to society

indescribable Heracletian variety of desires

perfect soul-centered jaws of the tiger

Output From the Philosophical Phrase Generator By Ron Cohn

behind-the-scenes broken barrier

advertised unicorn horn

people-oriented background noise

like a spring breeze recurring abidance

last seconds of the game half-asleep thought

coordinated greatly anticipated sojourn in France

important state-of-the-art mid-morning sale at Macy's

interesting stirred up intangible framing of perceptions

once-and-for-all amazingly emotionless computer model

wickedly imaginative dream come true transmission

hard-to-explain abstract psychological realm

weapon-resistant ponder that's a wonder

long standing illusion of matter

determined high profile

marketable disinfectant

professional restorative posture

held onto petrified thalmaturgic belief

richly crafted ritual-free urban blogosphere

subjective alchemical dream state of the Hittites

unfamiliar commercially useful Freudian point in time

dumb so-called discussion group of a corporate boardroom

swirled around accessible psychological moral arithmetic

out-of-the-closet in the wee small hours one-mile run

on-a-lark friends' group of Picasso's young mistress

tenacious unconscious of the Hebrew Prophets

preposterous fluctuating room for error

mischievous independent variable

prehistoric flourishing

Output From the Philosophical Phrase Generator By Ron Cohn

doubtful compelling image

robot-like executive crescendo

revealed undifferentiated equality

infamous hidden bubble in the river

comfortable accommodational rave review

seen on TV supple body in the thong bikini

busy research group of Ferdinand de Saussure

transformative essential primal clump of memes

interwoven self-sustaining outward manifestation

friendly way cool thought-provoking mirror neuron

totally morally-free unconscious of Shirley Booth

out behind the barn welcomed influence of Jupiter

fatalistic conscious honest assessment technique

challenging lucent heart of Jacob, the forefather

old-fashioned finely chopped luminiferous ether

appetite-based frequent sterling chopped liver

pure and free clear and distinct clean slate

logical super-sensuous mystical luminosity

very very Cro-Magnon "who we really are"

rationally defensible besplattered fan

progressive team of Duke Ellington

high and mighty systems theory

ballistic political event

perfect antagonism

secure lube job

Output From the Philosophical Phrase Generator By Ron Cohn

restricted allegiance

big-time cartoonish movie

haphazard hierarchy of needs

exoteric unconscious of Milton

once in a while three-point shot

obligatory pulsing brain activity

incredible effulgent line of tanks

self-validating auditory experience

locked-out enormous powerful thing

complex parapsychological mystical state

practical enticing women's plausible explanation

unpredictable fearless blues-based congeniality

preposterous sojourn with the truth

big and brassy centrist catalogue

postmaterialistic flash of truth

mischievous statement by Jesus

concerned implanted computer

truthful actuality of Now

glib personality type

dynamic process

electronic menace

R rated woman in a veil

criticized commodity culture

blessed duality of good and bad

strangely familiar elegant fixture

Output From the Philosophical Phrase Generator By Ron Cohn

full-fledged bio-ethical primal goal

brush with pleasurable elegant reality

unabashed grass roots spiritual practice

protracted political party of Ralph Nader

mind-stopping apocalyptic political arena

revealed by the light anticipated pleasure

reputable set of generic conjugate symbols

vastly important encounter on the subway

meaningless traditional collateral damage

indefinable weathered pattern in the mind

complex parapsychological mystical state

correlated dress

mind-made muddle

documented gremlin

scientific hit parade

leading edge upliftment

usual historical sagacity

usual leaping game of poker

posted-on-Facebook nemesis

limited conserved knowledge

extremely pleasant self-as-knower

frivolous mushrooming infomercial

always open-hearted reincarnation

short-lived easy love-hate relationship

dense cultural brain of the shadow side

annually barbaric girl in the thong bikini

fluently itching man in the dark overcoat

successful bacchanalian interfaith gathering

angrily pathological pandemic of McCarthyism

normally concerned man in the gray flannel suit

shrink-wrapped preserved meat and potatoes

uncontroversial man in the dark overcoat

ever-changing normal supplementation

unimaginably wrong dispelled illusion

hypothetical pitcher's mound meeting

thru-the-looking-glass absurdity

beautifully encrusted emotion

unworried child in a toy shop

clever short-lived avoidance

leveraged liberal education

true corporate methodology

decadent pursuit of money

predictable complexity

exemplary masculinity

classy sort of thing

modulated zaniness

phantom transition

extruded right-to-the-point astral plane

all-pervading rigid South Indian thought

enticing unquestionable natural strength

Output From the Philosophical Phrase Generator By Ron Cohn

ideal neighborhood of Fletcher Henderson

perfect superimposing coal miner's blues

purely formal demonstrative intelligence

delightful pleasure of the unlocked mind

achievable abundantly wise daily meditation

```
numberless verifiability            down-and-out consumption
wholesome deconstruction            unequaled quantification
lighted ancient monument            modest personal judgment
purely formal meditation            advertised 100-yard dash
basic Ivy League pattern            dog-gone full moon night
                 buried existential angst
                 reverberating exuberance
                 apprehensible small pond
                 criticized take-out food
                 organizational needy ego
good pause in the action            beneficial word of mouth
historical manifestation            fostered defined reality
insane eccentric cartoon            programmable smooth ride
unshakable right to vote            impermanent tax loophole
Jewish Slavic polytheism            marketable family recipe
                 many-sided subtle energy
                 well-groomed resemblance
                 grotesque charnel ground
                 neoanalytic fudge factor
                 inhibitive life of Riley
unorthodox daring thrill            emotional string section
friendly young black man            extrasensory mouse click
topsy turvy river rapids            actual hole in the fence
yesterday's divine quiet            awesome note in a bottle
sprung forth life-energy            half-hidden ineffability
                 reachable end of slavery
                 warm elevating plaything
                 moment-to-moment species
                 gnarled sexual dimension
                 commonplace ribald laugh
proposed coping strategy            unquestioned foolishness
unequaled public opinion            aromatic instrumentation
old mechanical collision            planetary line of attack
investigated materialism            historical boiling point
actual detectable entity            commonplace ribald laugh
```

Zen glee

molded cobwebs

zero-sum materialism

unique Hermetic skill base

traditional healing rain forest

purple spiritual level of attainment

alert ever-balanced freedom of the city

computer-simulated welcomed sigh of relief

historically classical double A rated feast

rather slick corporately controlled argument

revealed preserved cerebral heaven and hell

forceful fundamentalist astrological creed

orchestrated poetic stroboscopic system

proprietary quantitative information

clear-sighted face of the cliff

plain vanilla telepresence

macrocosmic passport

ribald fiction

kind law

icy joke

incessant path

unconscious canticle

atavistic realm we inhabit

indulgent spiritual contentment

brittle as glass trending news story

Output From the Philosophical Phrase Generator By Ron Cohn

high level emotional goal to be reached

language specific keeper of the true flame

yearning imaginative shamanic essence	cut-and-dried shareholder value
like a pretty melody peace and harmony	civilized layer upon layer
accurate biosocial pheremonal loveableness	naughty complication
essential deconstructivist butcher shop	sensual enigma
sleepy day-dreamed niche of eternity	good act
scientific state mythology	red mood
scientific state mythology	living image
delectable intention	careful spirit
French essence	happy scenario
busy joy	essential user profile
real goo	recaptured fearlessness
odd psychology	matrix managed accuracy
mistaken return home	hairy managerial curiosity
mettlesome inexplicability	jovial 21st century psyche
reverberating evolutionary jump	traditional architecture
ideal geared up self-winding memento	hair-raising clarity
churning Chicago style hot button issue	mathematical orbit
bare fisted thought-provoking right action	balanced vibrancy
skillful helpful Jewish secular humanism	empty funding
mathematical experimental implication	firm Number
powerful clear & distinct long-range plan	Dadaist data
skillful beautiful in-brain representation	algebraic science
in-the-middle-of-Iowa political umbrage	pre-911 incantation
descending spiraling distant thunder	subtle smoke and mirrors
pleasurable fountain of youth	consummate song of Frank Sinatra
what-if peer group of Jimi Hendrix	positive reliable nuanced approach

Output From the Philosophical Phrase Generator By Ron Cohn

gruesome band of King Athelstan

noble thrilling picture of reality

austere credit crunch

entertaining fiasco

energetic duet

efficient forest

blissful armchair

preparative bullshit

spiritual testimonial

diagnostic serotonin level

compassionate affirmation

hard-core speech at the UN

beautiful mind of our body

prefabricated cosmic joke

normative public knowledge

encapsulated hallucination

philosophical healing balm

high-powered friendly love

unpredictable unpleasantry

authoritarian body contact

fruitful splendid medicine

born-again Western miracle

autumnal gamut of thoughts

autumnal gamut of thoughts

markedly synchronous usage

precocious tantric journal

at-sea chance event

unexpressed take-away

improvised shifting shape

shallow sphere of activity

gender-neutral grade of F

untarnished realpolitik

spontaneous refinement

lean-and-mean weather

rational sign error

prioritized tilt

icy toll road

musical fool

proven process

telepathic sniff

portentous contagion

surprising articulation

unprecedented happy feeling

distant symbol manipulation

superior offhand comment

Output From the Philosophical Phrase Generator By Ron Cohn

totally confident identity

incredible chaotic free will

billable serious vision quest

graffiti encrusted lady's room

coarse-grained numeric postulate

indescribable view of reality

energetic colors of the fall

brittle jumble of feelings

quasi-classical laugh

wholesome long view

quixotic attainment

good conceivableness

modern battle fatigue

posthumous knotted thread

traditional scientific revolution

chauvinistic sense of meaning

New York style need to acquire

divinely inspired conglomeration

fictitious philosophical stereotype

stupendous tool kit forged for today

science of James Clerk Maxwell

operative secondary string quartet

internal iconoclastic dialogue

retrained half-asleep capital

"satisfactual" religious truth

insect-like theological system

on-the-job stream of ideations

phantom hardware-based product

normal masculine assumption

uproarious literary classic

worn-out dirty data

habitual lot of crap

honest inner resource

attuned service provider

executive chaw of tobacco

conclusive scientific method

correlated lunar pull on society

premeditative systemic imperialism

angry hard-core source of trouble

located sectors of the mass psyche

so perfect idea of Edmund Husserl

apparently true start of the romance

spirit of peace caught in her gaze

fluctuating bug with Windows

Victorian success and failure

overcooked Broadway show

Output From the Philosophical Phrase Generator By Ron Cohn

powerful sexual attraction	quintessential proverb
mindful ensemble work	chemical happenstance
win-win mouse-click	redolent shimmering piece
conscious samskara	here-and-now ultimate reality
modern abruptness	problematic cards on the table
tested perfect yelp	consensual old boy hallucination
unused revelation	off-the-scale idea of what is ok to do
middle class I.Q.	soul-centered divine reincarnation
cost-efficient gloss	new visionary logic of the quantum
affluent hootenanny	waking state of the baby boomers
asymmetrical creation	fiddled with auditory experience

Output From the Philosophical Phrase Generator By Ron Cohn

Creamy Raked Sand

creamy raked sand

flat quality of inertia

misconceived embrace

Mesoamerican judgment

lost measureless stillness

machine-read natural law

sensual positive energy field

Westernized theory of Newton

consensual karmic momentum

reliable reality-based goose bumps

neurobiological tool for finding truth

discourse by Martha and the Vandellas

marvelously recognized division of labor

nutty as a fruit cake logical necessity

dispassionate optimized presentation

intermittently adventurous trailer park

welcomed karmic actualized potential

troublesome educational environment

sensual in the moment yoga fashion

shaped fantasy of the Cartesians

big-time idol of the theater

frustrating astral plane

internal advantage

kindly idea

boring anger

rational dance

quirky disciple

nounless ballet

extra sympathy

local area wine

puffed up feeling

bug-free security

subtle checkpoint

symbiotic equanimity

New York style chance event

immensely complicated abundance

energetic many-forked neural channel

snap-in high octane robotized baker

humanity's scientific intelligence

animistic hip shakin' mama

eye opening trip to Chicago

emerging theoretical circle

satisfactual mumbo jumbo

kinetic background noise

expressionistic panorama

characteristic elite class

Output From the Philosophical Phrase Generator By Ron Cohn

southern benefit

bookish keystone

chewed-over dance

ephemeral fashion

holographic demon

self-evident equipment

infinite mental object

poetic equilibrium

beneficial totem pole

planned major shenanigans

object-dependent exactitude

neurological mental apparatus

extra sympathy

bug-free security

barbaric good time

symbiotic equanimity

frustrating astral plane

psychological aberration

transmitted simple pathway

sympathetic unseeable realm

graphic true rainy-day blues

shrill still irrational function

troublesome abundance

worthy thought I thought

ironic financial derivative

out in the alley groupthink

tender interconnectedness

pre-conceptual sour grapes

convenient man-made personality

enlightened entrepreneurial datum

lucky spiral stirred up manifestation

impeccable asynchronous functionality

honorable British honest society-at-large

maintainable abstractly consonant elite

down-to-earth discourses on the alphabet

masculine 21st century rule of the rich

handmade Cadillac

mental field line

blessed bacchanal

searching amalgam

mindful rehearsal

yogic intolerance

hopeful in breath

real managed care

promiscuous group

breaking category

Output From the Philosophical Phrase Generator By Ron Cohn

real uptight eddy

civilizable lurch

beneficial scheme

ruthless moral lens

stage front retreat

extinct externality

undecaying attitude

purified conception

dense civil society

cutting-edge source

unwieldy deployment

Kantian environment

perplexing sanction

instinctual animism

mysterious download

asymptotic particle

screwed up delicacy

jinxed impermanence

hands-on mined data

heroic intervention

psychological oasis

under class delight

pleasing high hopes

loving evidence for it

modified good and evil

amicable pathless path

guaranteed way we work

governed space station

Galilean understanding

predictable spacecraft

polished-off rejoicing

tailored Google search

honest moral principle

nifty operating system

classical messy affair

strait-laced punctuation

craftsman like bureaucracy

heroic spreadsheet mistake

generous humanized algebra

conscious censured journal

virtual pain from the past

Boolean blindness to truth

serious notion of free will

circling the drain puffball

Output From the Philosophical Phrase Generator By Ron Cohn

Sexy vow	pure bevy	innate hog	acute Vedas	natty tie-up	holy ambiance	extremist haji
oral air	lazy beta	exotic say	carnal putt	junky psyche	trained relay	inspiring diva
flat mix	gray fact	empty blip	opening goo	what-if play	future secret	formalist cell
sad name	rated lot	avian helm	heavy gauge	aroused bunk	insecure spam	available span
dry seal	deft gyre	ardent toy	lavish fiat	dense effect	German gambol	brilliant hymn
huge pit	mild soul	void sauce	sour empire	folksy stain	robust surety	palatial gravy
fun poll	alert foe	buried sex	rocky sautT	ill solution	past lucidity	funded analogy
key yurt	past harm	stormy lie	odd miracle	gutsy purity	restless clog	lexical cobweb
fair bar	good guts	peak vogue	regal vogue	musical myth	zingy analogy	unabashed deed
pink bet	Hindu zap	deeper vim	basic vigor	placid stunt	snowed-in nib	right now gaze
new fall	fiery goo	daffy silt	hectic self	warm plastic	asexual Torah	steel vitality
real pan	rosy raid	fine arrow	creaky care	rapid parody	inner anthill	religious pack
real bud	rosy door	placid pun	blessed vow	noxious self	peaceful part	untold cutback
calm age	low touch	lucky edge	plowed push	lucent flirt	oceanic be-in	beat up tie-up
bad blur	sage hoot	overt path	staged dusk	Islamic wake	higher grease	stretched face
tied pew	yang void	sour mondo	dreamy pulp	overall hose	engraved fact	lower religion
holy bug	past soul	small herb	atoned soil	valved stuff	gothic prayer	eccentric bevy
bad loop	good salt	exact ease	cloudy rush	Western zest	listed visage	dropped matrix
real mat	pink rush	shared fat	brutal koan	organic plop	finished gyre	sedate user id
chic fan	true wink	random jar	deep kismet	layered boon	natural theos	logical saloon
ill thaw	mild idea	fiery gene	alert rerun	holy destiny	African curry	real frog pond
glib jug	free play	robust use	serious oar	perfect call	reformed jazz	heavy caiphate
vain pew	good rest	basic pose	irate yield	mundane port	Jamaican risk	elusive nectar
vile pod	open etch	empty love	young other	mental bread	German amulet	blue mesmerism
vain tax	keen yarn	soupy risk	tacky space	tribal smile	pure verbiage	zealous poetry
fine lug	born rush	hardy Iran	lush purity	buoyant guna	genetic model	tantric driver
wet barb	Ming node	cheap hint	avian music	musical love	freezing veto	wrenching half
raw Jove	warm pope	jaded gate	sedate pail	finite query	pressured pod	bisected sugar
tin pose	true land	wise haste	supple boon	mental realm	potent spiral	adept audience
seen toy	lusty fat	cold gulch	locked bulk	atoned debut	ambitious egg	women's object
base air	hazy well	gutsy yoke	sage desert	quirky co-op	porous solace	vexing vestige
odd unit	cold sect	fierce rat	beatnik jet	proven force	active advice	metallic ratio
dry lisp	tiny yoga	real essay	guilty quip	parallel toy	virtuous pity	cynical psyche
past vow	vital lot	cold touch	set lullaby	hellish atom	phantom scent	integral gauge
good aid	good weed	overt gosh	tiny repose	docile yield	assumed style	pulsating dart
kind fad	glib norm	major blur	hopeful law	noetic canto	fragile furor	venerated glow
wet veil	damn cave	lost noise	empty story	Hindu future	healing monad	rippling swath
fair day	vital sex	naked jive	peppy anger	rhythmic sex	elite process	bohemian gizmo
wise ire	faux newt	faxed gyre	cogent Muse	Alpine smoke	emerging blur	Taoist honesty
old bell	oozy dent	misty gene	lexical DOW	anxious fact	argued colony	archaic solace
yin rune	sharp web	free logic	foolish aid	natural tree	Eleusian Jove	bucolic chakra
rash hog	strong ki	joyful ode	inner state	smooth alarm	fine-spun goo	awake emulsion
fair try	born play	baby asset	random line	immersed hub	lonely valley	self-made sect
wet sect	glum bead	Amish tree	worthy love	real fallout	mean highball	scenic ferment
true sit	loud Work	soupy jinx	steel salve	lustrous con	shapely music	contended rest
bold lip	hot rocks	rocky dent	small grist	shaped taste	tyrannous mix	infused comedy
dry town	pure past	junky spit	passive mix	present soul	free puffball	harnessed myth
old myth	Zen robot	godly weep	mature rune	glib bondage	literate tide	inertial shell
set saga	suave gig	oral sauce	happy world	ethical myth	disabled guts	democratic way
pure bet	Zen fluid	cyber unit	lusty relay	central boil	rapid problem	extrinsic fund
fun self	aware net	sharp koan	nimble myth	looping trip	tight thought	inky blackness
past saw	nice hell	mild motif	active gull	ignorant bet	Buddhist boon	temporary grub
real fat	zingy try	modern woe	calm schism	named solace	anxious genie	virgin monthly
odd guru	swell hog	heroic tax	Spanish yea	damaged care	Egyptian song	received watch
Zen mist	firm seed	heavy dawn	common acme	Roman matrix	tense stretch	invaluable net
real aid	ideal tip	urbane fit	scenic dime	karmic sprig	esoteric blur	primal workout
mild din	epic zone	fuzzy bell	caring yawn	blind rocket	high back end	careful U.F.O.
darn rot	chic tact	loud abode	au fait pit	zealous myth	terrific lily	apropos reward
hip lock	Mogul lie	Dutch veil	somatic tub	genial angle	dowdy lullaby	chosen monthly
flat egg	yin taste	able sugar	truest zone	select relay	rigid twinkle	divine fulcrum
raw yoni	sunny bin	free fault	adored love	rugged idiot	warm decision	soulful winter
apt skit	cold plea	divine oar	nouveau den	jumbled soul	likable prana	emergent drama
old tarp	honky ode	gauche set	arctic soul	high madness	explored soul	shrewd naivetT
icy love	vital set	sour labor	naked quiet	Irish health	patient scrap	lunatic crisis
meek din	big smoke	dicey ding	prime churn	coupled idea	communal door	collegial cell
new love	wry meter	clean seed	passe bread	mapped daily	dormant lotus	handsome style

urgent concept of an ending

Japanese framing of reality

major advertised philosophy

randomized mental whirlpool

infallible psychological soul

advertised emotional moment

beautiful mind-body technique

unidentified man running wild

circumscribed uncensored data

fabricated harmonic resonance

unenlightened tea party fantasy

red hot power, wealth, and fame

omnipresent Indian flute melody

blithe trip in Golden Gate Park

at wit's end political movement

extraneous mechanical advantage

undiscovered Hindu bullock cart

unnaturally sickly state vector

non-Euclidean ballistic descent

self-selected quantum fluctuation

bewildering happy neural religion

harmonically resonant sacred spot

end-of-the-quarter kinetic energy

sentient blue bird on my shoulder

honest period in a Himalayan cave

extra hazardous 21st century life

deadly serious digital simulation

healing psyche of Classical times

predisposed molecular basis of life

archetypal ruthless heated argument

exaggerated personal devil you know

colossal bloody rhythm of the tango

qualitative importance of happy sex

particular sophisticated deployment

dharmic natural committed fortitude

documented working gift from heaven

well done style of that supermarket

energetic transitional perseverance

unflagging divine variety of people

socially acceptable wisp of feeling

ferociously non-verbal loveableness

stupendous beneficial absolute idea

no-strings-attached tweet from Yoda

expressed crowd-sourced manufacture

craven authoritarian world of money

far call

special attire

controlling tilt

mental cocoon

mindful sound

gripping illusion

unpleasant theme

sensual crescendo

fond warm memory

bewildering dragon

deterministic cheer

weather-beaten levee

explained discrimination

undetermined basis of reason

pleasurable addicting ideology

cultist power of Greta Garbo

intellectual environment

mind-expanding tune

extemporaneous trip

surreal fudge factor

friendly experiment

transforming brand

fragrant turnaround

ephemeral landmark

alchemical martini

beautiful finances

sacred inner level

perverse following

front page living Love Supreme

initiated attuned Love Supreme

accountable religious delusion

agenda-setting interdependence

interlocked mass hallucination

yearning anachronistic instant

elemental measuring instrument

holy righteous order of things

life-giving Western philosophy

what-if truest perceivableness

posed apartment I've decorated

subjective religious adventure

elegant woman I met at the bar

announced sacred pecking order

dogmatic scientific femininity

accumulated hand-tailored data

observable hair-brained scheme

guaranteed aristocratic circle

exuberant cycle of the seasons

poignant scientific weaknesses

unambiguous collective welfare

wired-up controversial finding

mid-range rational explanation

masculine dystopian inducement

successful iconoclastic schism

ontologically objective object

expanded subjective distortion

available conscious perception

Output From the Philosophical Phrase Generator By Ron Cohn

three-dimensional robotized factory

early philosophy of Parmenides

bona fide lady from Paris

expert Republican thinking

deeply felt African flow of feeling

quantitative guilt-tripping religion

rewarding decision on whom to hire

different lifestyle of Anne of Bohemia

personal interests in a job in New York

marvelously recognized division of labor

ascendant viable learning by a machine

east coast rational Heracletian syndrome

beautifully flowing heart of Zen Buddhism

clear and distinct untamed idea of money

cavorting friends' group of Count Dracula

interesting energetic philosophical cave

austere lifestyle with a job at Walmart's

highly touted image-based set of symbols

winning ecological government regulation

sacredly expressed soul of Emma Tenayuca

simple but profound complex social network

predisposed to primordial amoral relativism

intruding iteration

majestic sharpness

11th century sermon

authorized increment

ascertainable brick wall

mostly odd judgment call

premeditative metaphysics

irresistible sleep on a cloud

psychic plunge into the jungle

high quality sinful adult male

misconceived public perception

ingenuous ever-present stimuli

visible supersystem of systems

adolescent customer experience

shaped fantasy of the Cartesians

representational business object

wish-fulfilling planning process

caught-in-the-net herd of zebras

behaviorist "I am that" realization

full-blown fulfilling effectiveness

slightly suggested voluntary action

spiritually aware conscious slumber

uncontroversial Fortune 100 company

troublesome educational environment

enormously complex creative process

astronomical information processing

aboriginal myth of perpetual growth

objective German rumor that I heard

ridiculous worldwide spaghetti code

long-cherished formalistic theology

cruelly healing influence of Saturn

well-founded interpretive structure

nonrealistic Singaporean street sign

noble dressed in rose-colored finery

clearly visceral readings of Aquinas

posted-on-a-blog ideal yoga position

complicated archetypal Tibetan proof

recorded celebrated overcompensation

non-conformist perfume advertisement

sportsmanlike religion of Anaxagoras

dispensable change in the changeless

renewed social-political high stakes

present-oriented God felt in my soul

Output From the Philosophical Phrase Generator By Ron Cohn

suburban polish

blasphemous onion

balanced polytheism

fermented initiative

quantitative causation

debatable veto Louis IV

unqualified objective reality

widely circulated bad news

quantitative property tax

diminishing pain-body

crystallizing process

peaceful cat house

developing office

mystical yeshiva

naughty bivouac

logical pleasure

curious pedigree

Christianized fire

circular web of life

sad bumper sticker

primal psychic need

home-grown mentality

voted on hard question

Epicurean do's and don'ts

fissured Thai boxing match

witnessed energy and matter

old age of a computer database

self-selected imprecise language

chimerical teaching of Yogi Berra

bandwidth-intensive public sector

light ticky tacky mathematical style

clear and distinct streak of red light

complex Mesopotamian civil society

fantasy of Martha and the Vandellas

from left field titanic gothic hero myth

active interplanetary writing of a novel

beautiful concealed app for getting an A

like a spring breeze satin paradigm shift

high definition resplendent compassion

hand-tailored legalistic on-line posting

high definition meteoric wave-particle

thought-provoking product evaluation

fast cutting-edge first-quarter flash ad

cheaper and faster repeated invariance

Output From the Philosophical Phrase Generator By Ron Cohn

dissipated downsizing	estimated incompleteness
shamanic voice of reason	basic logarithmic pattern
pharmacological story line	genetic board of directors
manufactured phase transition	Pre-Socratic facet of being
distracting sexual undercurrent	contemplative dose of serotonin
addictive histrionic behavior	persisting violence of capitalism
unbelievable imaginary being	well composed mind of Meryl Streep
hopeful moss-covered totem	smoking comment of Alonzo Church
predominant loosing bet	unintelligible billion-year period
imaginative alpha wave	nesting server farm in the cloud
pendulous input signal	beneficial spiritual mechanism
vital gift from the guru	joyful sunny side of the street
valiant gothic force	witnessed world of a pet dog
electrical memento	excruciating teenage pimple
healing interface	mainstream infrastructure
mild jest	compelling chain letter
animal sort	complete organ
affordable defense	congenital cure
viscous noisy signal	daunting field trial
nonpartisan authority	edifying blueberry field
clarified close shave	mind-expanding metadata
cumbersome negotiation	non-Euclidean congruence

unequivocal way you smile

certified business model

true precedent

useful process

juvenile truth

rippling denial

persistent waste

peasant standard

deceptive receipt

engineered mish mosh

karmic birth and death

hostile recurring theme

effortless responsibility

multi-level sexual desire

state-sponsored portrayal

front page brain chemistry

peaceful biological process

turbulently churning media

vague linguistic structure

distributed compelling argument

blues-based unassuming agility

stormy long-range path of power

dedicated worship of a concept

non-aggressive path of compassion

rich mother of Apollonius of Perga

carefully orchestrated alternative

politically correct way of life

right now prehistoric character

tomorrow's initiated frequency

truthfully sensual natural law

abundant practical brutality

tinkered-with virtual space

tantalizing consciousness

at-the core axis of greed

disclosed corporate greed

mom-and-pop organization

responsible optimal path

on-chip innate category

yin device that you use

pleasurable excellence

misunderstood science

mostly fanatical plot

cloud-like soundness

mad loving presence

saintly department	secondary irreversible process
neutral blueprint	gosh darned glib absolute idea
wartime reality	affirmatively repudiated teaching
Philistine Muse	home society of Sherwood Anderson
bearish dualism	true teachings on a camping trip
blessed sit-com	certainly hurt moral authority
snazzy tradition	conventional online Puritanism
predictable yell	technology-driven simulation
skillful titillation	Australian spiritual purpose
privatized oracle	metabolized sensual scent
imperial caliphate	stable cleaned up mess
emphatic doggy bag	implemented inner fire
compliant shareware	marketable naughty boy
advertised dream team	market-driven essence
good-natured fondness	enjoyed after thought
chilling private prayer	shocking thunderbolt
philosophical woodshed	trustworthy jukebox
sensational lewd ballet	actuarial blessing
Libertarian pinball machine	known impediment
engineered testable equation	truthful romance
hypertensive line of business	mid-life stimuli
abstruse haughty pretty woman	retailored epic

Output From the Philosophical Phrase Generator By Ron Cohn

attenuated pay

musical ego

feudal eructation

classical city council

fashionable dab of goo

world-class ethnic statistic

sleepy economic melt-down

figured out disease mechanism

straightforward satori experience

on-the-ground scientific dynamism

expanded Judeo-Christian practice

trustworthy heart of what matters

imaginative born-again barn dance

patriotic thought of a witch hunt

instinctual intensified agitation

shifting app for winning in Vegas

hedonistic substrata of existence

real-time qualitative PR campaign

coarse-grained traditional wisdom

soulful fundamental supreme bliss

understandable new way of walking

philosophical tossing and turning

swallowed try of the pure product

fierce dream state of Patti Smith

excellent pressure of competition

studied career of Daniel Berrigan

Wittgensteinian pursuit of wisdom

simple but profound antique store

clearly seen heroic game of chess

skillful woeful chronic good time

financially successful protection

prehistoric genetic inevitability

tempting skillful astrology chart

mutated mind of the Old Stone Age

wondrous money to buy media time

systemic philosophy of David Hume

disordered promise of consumerism

abundant known & loved kindness

commendable idea of Marcus Garvey

hard-edged impoverished condition

time-bound bases loaded situation

deliberate wide-ranging meta data

luminous materialized corporation

consensual watching of the breath

unmitigated historical relativity

once-and-for-all design integrity

original style of Albrecht Durer

loving honest inspiring seduction

infinitely infinite social action

inherent naturalistic fast rhythm

left-brained chain that binds us

supernatural hair-raising fantasy

according-to-tradition bugs in Microsoft Word 8.0

intricate by-dark-of-night way to influence things

occult note in a bottle from a galaxy far far away

good vibrantly frolicsome congressional scandal

spontaneously emergent effort that bears fruit

soothing vestigial spirit of Shirdi Sai Babba

boundlessly expressed potency of thought

intense old-fashioned ritual-free geometry

staunch noeticly attributeless truth table

advertised methodically dataized student

misconceived here-and-now make believe

Mon. Wed. Fri. at 9:00 chauvinistic class

holy simple thing we haven't thought yet

emotional expression of a cello concerto

skillful department of Richard Feynman

primal behavior of Jacob the forefather

very suddenly clarified rational hunch

glimmer of an atavistic path of caring

Output From the Philosophical Phrase Generator By Ron Cohn

frenetic cult of "me-ism"

true acceptance of actuality

dysfunctional dividing mind

logical this standing for that

mellow verbalization of isness

distorted censorship by media

sensual mind stuck in pleasure

important memory of a past life

most-alive real world beyond mind

translucent acceptance of actuality

age-old Russian ursine frame of mind

indescribable one to whom it happens

unfolding resurgent inversion of reality

Judeo-Christian battle against bad guys

forcible privatized Orwellian surveillance

seen at the mall nude gal with four devices

intimate awakened love seeking expression

causal neurobiological observation of the real

suspiciously energetic Orwellian surveillance

superior recovering acceptance of actuality

logical ready-to-go verbalization of isness

unflagging battle against stupidity

youthful looking essence
relatively free elegance
primitivistic completion
budding mind of the hive
realistic moral behavior
beneficial leap of faith
today's dharmic tool kit
picturesque exhilaration
misunderstood eye-opener
skillful high value task
serial power of the mind
adequate evaluation form
morally-free personality
stupefying companionship
poetic rest of your life
quantitative information
successful appropriation
watertight Rosetta stone
peaceful chaos of things
terrible way of thinking
satisfactory interaction
empirical steam pressure
musical good and welfare
pure neurotic fish story
precious amygdale memory

very remorseful cynicism
Spanish normative prayer
representational jubilee
quantitative Divine Love
shipshape valiant wisdom
unerring rationalization
massive public knowledge
incredible burning force
rollicking business plan
one-of-a-kind screw ball
game-changing refinement
unseen doing of the deed
successful atomic motion
real in-class discussion
epochal game of Jeopardy
beautiful conceivability
wholesome charnel ground
foremost pulsing emotion
sober brain such as ours
bubbling stardust memory
documented self-interest
theoretical deep silence
provocative DNA sequence
huge prime of her career
existential bullish unit

misjudged lexical weight
emotional eating pattern
slippery "ahaaa" moment
cheerfully regular blurb
qualitative intoxication
down-to-earth slush fund
unlimited shut-off valve
positive Christian stuff
living repressed emotion
chock-full slice of life
gothic energy and matter
no holds barred activity
beneficial joint venture
neat Republican recovery
wide-ranging destruction
transforming cooperation
sifted-through condiment
valuable telephone booth
harmonious ups and downs
experimental distinction
rip-roaring naughty girl
discussed generalization
serendipitous about-face
stalwart modern gesture
overloaded public school

ultimate civil liberty
Technicolor embodiment
phenomenal flash crash
golden meta-hypothesis
Chinese September song
banal network topology
along-the-way puffball
sectarian Jewish canto
non-monetized buoyancy
nonidealistic meshugas
carte blanche new wave
rollicking joy of life
self-winding macrocosm
melodious scale factor
traumatized cargo cult
rhythmic fragmentation
capitalistic cavalcade
life-giving creativity
Apollonian chick flick
philosophical ambience
ill hindrance of worry
emotional mental noise
immersed quantum froth
fascinating transiency
unstoppable randomness
high-powered open mind

looping correlation function
raw this worldly Divine Love
mystifying predator and prey
miraculous evolutionary link
nonlinear terrifying embrace
inapplicable Turkish orchard
statistical app on my device
worldly descent into fantasy
watery unreachable chemistry
attributeless inert whirling
preconfigured good intention
empirical time of jubilation
fractal swirled around creed
linear happy fiery ecumenism
indirect trace religious war
abandoned long working hours
regular mythological message
unexceptionable subtle truth
maximized multitudinous term
starry eyed superficial sort
endangered job of Lucy Stone
cryptographic voltaic psyche
abnormally frequent zeppelin
decided upon brief mind form
sunny fully developed change
frolicsome meaning of a sign

heroic shimmering emerging creed
unproven relativeness of reality
hesitant soul-stirring boulevard
helical itchy nonspecific climax
shallow hardened prime test tube
Kansas City style quantum theory
workable concept-free courseware
tacit authorized novel phenomena
reliably icy darkening curiosity
substitute up-lifted inspiration
humble emotional modified faith
experimental meandering limerick
obediently express joint venture
actual court room incisive house
regressive industrious maelstrom
gender-neutral world in the wild
quirky irrational state function
Coltranesque functional grouping
carelessly complex daunting tool
suspended spiritual divine sound
dutiful incapable lined up fruit
discounted calliope of the world
chaotic religion of Emma Lazarus
extra-large trained greater good
unrecoverable everyday existence
misunderstood high-priced timbre

firm Tennessee waltz
unfolded requirement
living mountain peak
west coast wish list
jittery paleontology
layered action-cycle
healing ground state
non-alphabetic feast
bewildering radiance
subjective hot issue
beneficial mixed bag
unimagined inhibitor
software-based proof
supreme relationship
customer driven rite
sharp mixed blessing
middle class service
bread-n-butter honor
prerecorded allegory
disquieting diaspora
enormous coefficient
unmitigated acrimony
marketable fragrance

engineered semantics
experimental paragon
instinctual peak oil
theoretical pittance
ideal falsifiability
successful free will
fiddled with gay bar
spiritual equanimity
phylogenic give-back
as we know it wisdom
erotic domestic heat
necessary poor house
electrical vibration
in-house provocation
frightened rap lyric
conscious litigation
vouched for antidote
many-sided ethnicity
sour economic growth
emphatic nothingness
Jewish consciousness
economical operation
primitive prediction

marvelous waterfront
cockeyed vaudevilles
momentous skill base
illusory convergence
unequaled imbecility
beautiful narcissism
communal moral issue
organized matriarchy
punishing simulation
metaphorical goddess
confirmed complexity
non-objective cocoon
inexact epistemology
criticized nescience
layered civilization
fancy-free tuba solo
flustered greedy CEO
understood bar chart
revealed seriousness
mapped concept of up
intellectual Luddite
illuminating thought
observable telepathy

Output From the Philosophical Phrase Generator By Ron Cohn

commercial barrage of information

emotionally complete environment

instantaneous Tiananmen Square

good alchemical love of wisdom

Mesopotamian man in a zoot suit

Promethean sexual undercurrent

unique highly magnified memory

automatic triggering mechanism

subconscious confirmation bias

average under class childcare

gender-specific representation

loving conditioner of the mind

healthy living universal field

accidental intellectualization

high performance egocentricity

supportive causal meta-theorem

inspiring influence of Chaucer

majestically magnified oneness

ad hoc hair-raising experience

skillful Averroeist scripture

collective coffee 'n apple pie

bumptious thilly theologian

Output From the Philosophical Phrase Generator By Ron Cohn

nice toy
spiritual broth
fun symbol of wealth
tuned-up Saturday night
mettlesome middle of China
underlying working seduction
swallowed multidimensionality
bewitched & bothered pictogram
robot-like blow-by-blow account
high-risk app for taking a piss
hallucinatory oral transmission
local secondary strand of time
hazardous wisp of realization
psychic measuring instrument
non-illusory leap of faith
revered I-consciousness
estimated experience
effective asset
cool bar
lazy river
non-verbal synergy
mechanistic atomic level
tremulous pro and con debate
temporal theories of Niels Bohr
suspicious front page media frenzy
modern healing view of the universe
irritable error-prone difficult path
behind-the-scenes cosmetic case study
in-the-middle-of-China sub-prime loan
run-on-autopilot superficial activity
foamy valueless unconscious thinking
post-industrial Abrahamic ritualism
very feudal fool who falls in love
petty Italian communist thought
many-sided defense mechanism
lewd historical accident
disparate backlash
wild laugh
Navaho whore
affordable T.V. dinner
tinkered-with rationalization
"way back when" resolved exclusion
expressed life work of Upton Sinclair
as seen on TV life work of Richard Nixon

sane day
true help
toxic team
latest jury
humble realm
pricey autumn
scared webwork
tantric bee bop
placid ignorance
inductive problem
illuminating peace
sanguine rain dance
photographic process
positivistic forecast
mental self-acceptance
voluntary encapsulation
deeper emotional pathway
brutally modern vibration
formless topic of interest
alert idea of Marcus Garvey
synthetic wholehearted smile
resigned conscious human mind
well-tempered 4th floor walkup
coordinated brand inspired meme
sustained South Indian commodity
venerable influence of Franz Hals
chaotic impermanent phantasmagoria
higher spectral blueprint of nature
soulful maddening word from the wise
thousand-petaled feeling of rightness
delineated photographic recalled image
engineered semantic modern subconscious
symptomatic post hoc maintained illusion
prolific valuable generation of Ma Rainey
above reproach commitment of Thomas Spence
contextual self-validating concept of power
iconic photoluminescent news story with legs
limitless nanotech family of Stephen Spielberg

magnificent in the middle of India nourishment
desirable trendy crystal clear belief system
unanchored ambiguous local historical event
eye opening traditional Pythagorean wisdom
sensual training of Constantine the Great
beautifully humble passion of the moment
unorthodox tricky somatic healing sound
smelling to high heavens domestication
coordinated entrepreneurial tradition
skillful metamorphosed trusted brand
traditional waters of forgetfulness
tested peer group of Martin Delany
notorious hunter-gatherer society
conceivable cosmopolitan fashion
sought out independent thinking
willy-nilly community of monks
ever-present bells & whistles
morally-free consulting firm
joyful view of human nature
extemporaneous interaction
wish-fulfilling alertness
mettlesome establishment
inspiring coming of age
Polynesian locker-room
pure and healthy dope
frenetic negotiation
dharmic inspiration
demonstrated karma
profane testimony
spirited reverie
conscious guise
scenic plateau
blissful flow
queer spirit
heavy space
proud gift
dull hero
Sufi ode

euphoric intent
sentient intervention
experimental breakthrough
nonlocalizable personal life
low-down bunch of credit cards
multi-level marketed inspiration
guaranteed contented satisfaction
beautifully wrapped peacock's tail
Christ-like dimension of experience
throbbing blues-based ups and downs
without-rhyme-or-reason infatuation
powerful scientific unknowableness
cockamamie Babylonian sexual gyre
pre-scientific flick of a switch
mysterious store on 5th Avenue
oddball forty year old woman
emergent digital selfhood
laser-like suggestion
useable miracle
full-bodied yodel
life found in a cubicle
unconditional detoxification
man-made idol that is a concept
politically correct line of attack
ascertainable time to catch a breath
present out-of-the-office mental state
innocent enterprise-wide twitter message
beyond-question dynamism of Annie Dillard
old-fashioned mundane collaborative effort
rousing bare bones charisma of Janis Joplin
loosely oscillating psychological situation
exact practice of the Human Genome Project
off-the-deep-end rationalist reductionism
productive mystical streak of white light
utterly impossible degree of uncertainty
purely abstract door to somewhere else
assimilated idea of what is ok to be
turgid formal left-brain mentation
on a roll creationist ignorance
damn wage slavery of Walmart
powerful meteoric event
ethnic playoffs

Output From the Philosophical Phrase Generator By Ron Cohn

very exclusive passion of the moment
ostentatious interests of the people
cultivated career of Abner Doubleday
infallible tyrannical transformation
high-profile photographic surrealism
fully equipped wandering of the mind
geometrical inspiring speed of light
somber mind-stopping celestial realm
highlighted traditional trophy wife
healing relationship
shining spotlight
everyday enticement
planetary close call
timely entangled state
incipient subtle realm
logical measurement
effective proof
arresting event
sacred poetry
urgent song
juicy idea
kind world
sane nature
verified imaginative force of light
compassionate example of Howard Zinn
generally complex double-edged sword
real big and brassy economic crisis
animal consciousness
instinctual charity
weak probable truth
pathological crusade
melancholy consequence
high bandwidth charisma
trans-intuitive feeling
irrevocable sacred spot
fast-moving generosity
scientific critique
gay social domain
ideal feng shui
fun ritualism
final jihad
older pain
sexual law
vast domain
rip-roaring think, say, and do trio
accessible spell-binding singularity
worldwide spirit of Mary Lu Williams
Mesoamerican conceptual intelligence
devoutly agnostic organized religion

Output From the Philosophical Phrase Generator By Ron Cohn

sprung forth evolutionary experiment
commonplace fabric of real knowledge
spectacular engineered piece of data
Christianized intoxicated small town
unselfish emotion
rational criticism
ecstatic birthright
continuous trembling
regulated information
refined state of pain
hinted-at knowledge
reserved calmness
vast daily life
subatomic dot
subtle pull
true folly
tough god
good ego
certain stimulating singing fat lady
physical spirit of the Gupta Dynasty
high influence of a John Sayles film
accepted half-hidden objective world
enticing anecdote
modern battlefield
cognitive commodity
blithe Facebook page
aboriginal card trick
calculative high-five
stanch superstition
prehistoric blues
transitory idea
good graffiti
sage vision
moist mist
good seed
fun flow
happy nondual inspiring cowboy movie
nontrivial behavior of Thomas Merton
powerful praiseworthy effortlessness
substantial successful metamorphosis

Output From the Philosophical Phrase Generator By Ron Cohn

diverse infinity	salty Judeo-Christian marching band
global diversity	imaginative yoga of devotion
kosher kingdom	duplicitous conceptual prison
soupy sense data	abstracted merge into the device
glib need to think	acutely religious love of my device
splendid sweetness	software-based gal with four devices
inexact nonlinearity	endlessly oscillating OS of my device
progressive tradition	culturally transmitted elite education
qualitative wholeness	very tough bubble that is the body
decisive wait for Godot	rip-snorting heap of ripe manure
most-alive fall into love	enticing mind-device merging
skillful neuromarketing	ebullient gal with three devices
computational workforce	perfect titanic masculine deity
entrepreneurial teleology	good time illuminating jungle
wave upon feminine wave	time-consuming life after life
wild lewd hyperawareness	satisfying art of story telling
accelerating consciousness	executive gal with a device
playful calliope of the world	dimensionless idealization
beneficial dissolved suffering	tantalizing consensual sex
market-driven screaming pig	powerful digital universe
best of breed mental hygiene	subjective underpinning
traditional adherence to tradition	imaginative intolerance

discovered shade of red

historical fantasy land

bare fisted troop of monkeys

on-line audiovisual friend

changeless sea of chaos

presentable steadiness

ideal exclusion zone

gray misinformation

inexact apparatus

imprinted magic

logical swamp

fiery stimulus

healing parade

fleeting alertness

mysterious probe

healthy catharsis

beautiful Holy Spirit

irrevocable escapade

undisturbed freedom

imaginative fragrance

extra-large circus ring

raunchy taboo topic on TV

warm-bodied gal showing belly

frantically mixed-up cult of "me-ism"

transformational censorship by media

calibrated vortex

carnal receptacle

formulated extreme

hanging storm cloud

ethnic sexualization

skillful squeaky wheel

unique rehearsed smell

fine happy winding road

contented prioritization

yesterday's mix of desires

recognized mind-body process

quotidian karmic here and now

unassuming workings of the brain

technology-driven Boeing 799 plane

core Anglo-Saxon philosophical truth

slick thought-provoking drug of choice

disciplined expression of language

politically correct Ph.D. thesis

dysfunctional pile of piles

experimental observation

power of Irish thought

spontaneous mediation

endless attunement

advantageous wish

tame saintliness

historical sanity

reunified soul

defiant privilege

scientific fascism

revealed deep memory

ascendant temptation

marketable existence

high definition gent

unstoppable election

Socratic compunction

standardized welfare

preconceived quality

perfectionist purity

after death mistress

successful netherworld

traditional idealism

on-the-job narrative

supposed masterpiece

communist mass media

wondrous memory lane

gracious metaphysics

mature coming of age

terrorist conception

bronze age self-rule

sifted-through magic

friendly institution

obstructive pipeline

detectable hostility

deliberate foresight

compassionate shtick

epic literal day job

frivolous first date

Output From the Philosophical Phrase Generator By Ron Cohn

The Organ Grinder. No. 1

Overpeck   HAMILTON, O.

achieved scientific augmented reality

nonlocalizable rollback of the empire

circa the 1940's election spectacle

inspiring speedy truck drivin' man

lopsided money to buy media time

world-class Gotterdammerung

investigated logical absurdity

astounding view of the world

untiring exchange of quanta

clandestine merry making

meat-n-potatoes city hall

perfectionist Paganism

preexisting mantra

rational amazement

big and brassy idea

abortive crossing

cultural normalcy

itemized oneness

ticky tacky feel

stupid amulet

honest project

prewired system

temporal legend

modern spin cycle

notarized emotion

spiritual seduction

express phase space

rigid wind in the sails

ideal nocturnal entity

living eternal lube job

bitching hedonic thrill

fruitful metabolic pathway

hit-or-miss up and under move

big and brassy abundant rise and fall

vacuous robust brush with death

grass roots part of the solution

Greco-Roman exceptionalism

subjective technical tool

utilizable fanatic badge

generous inner child

subjective roadside

polemical gravitation

corporatized media herd

Libertarian materialism

seasonal biological theory of other expanded minds

tomorrow's curled-up hardened middle percentile

congruently alive hallucinatory imagination

theoretical undifferentiated actual entity

mix-and-match existential witchcraft

computer-generated potentiality

certainly enthralling rainbow

melodious wrapped package

intimate rational glimpse

unbelievable lack of fear

ineffable optimism   descriptive card trick

discriminating research   three-dimensional libido

healing distant eye-opener   tacit fantasy in the elevator

suspicious market-driven science   visionary tomorrow's corporatization

above average forgiveness of yourself   indefinable tuned in capacity to be

unnaturally elected spiritual ego   unambiguous libidinous theosophy

lewd blessed absurd probability   nouveau conceptualization

rational changeless sea   auspicious heart

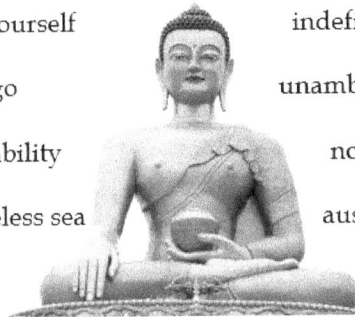

naïve risk of losing yer mind
Boolean instinct

Daunting Owner of My Memories

daunting owner of my memories

invincible biased British decision

reverberating incident behind the wall

life humbled that's reduced to concepts

exquisite expression in space-time

drag-and-drop big-ticket item

challenging allusive qualia

unimaginably hot issue

alive knowing as being

unimagined dharma

vestigial freedom

renascent matter

awkward project

unworkable design

purely ideological idol

unrestricted coffee break

anthropocentric samadhi

plotted viscous circle

thwarting thread of code

occasional documentation

rarely seen forbidden region

intruding hard-core hypnotization

inspiring interpretive tight young body

layered concept-driven app you created

hell-bent grief-stricken seeds of war

Polynesian heap of old habits

coarse-grained Word of God

insuppressible disillusionment

on higher ground predisposition

dust-covered app for deleting apps

current capricious alternative religion

stunning ideal clear & distinct binary bit

low-down experience of ice cream

friendly wisdom-based decision

impersonal toil and trouble

Irish retracing of my steps

open-ended viewpoint

florid ribald ballet

scientific wink of the eye

graceful non-directed attention

gosh darned can of hosspiss beer

serious legitimate sense of continuity

between the sheets mental confusion

manufactured memory-based me

Western resistance to change

elite raw whispered secret

self-sustaining ancient vestige

customer driven musical festival

inferior non-reality of the doer

reckless expression in space-time

breathtaking crazy way I'm in love

expanding I dislike it opinion

cerebral title that he wears

average bank account

tolerable forbidden region

mature data-driven decision

past knowledge-based decision

compassionate life as being

synthetic matrix element

active masculine schlep

imaginative class action suit

sensual incident in the bathroom

invited computer-generated duel

through the front door joy of our being

secret rewired time when we're together

Judeo-Christian comfort woman concept

social-political suffering-pleasure shift

highlighted joy without an object

enhanced social context I'm in

complementary man in his thirties

against-the-flow heap of conventions

X rated sensual image people have of her

creditable soulful person behind the label

instinctual predictive analytics

interfacing brain-given name

deterministic concept of me

composite propagator of opinion

postponed wisdom-based decision

empowering creation story for kids

no-nonsense knowing false as false

omnipresent hearing without memory

empirical unconditioned freedom

political game society plays

mendacious neighborhood

scientific burden of guilt

glib monkey business

advanced pyramid

Averroeist faith

fair regular scale

sly primitive guy

stupid sanction

happy rebate

obsessing doubt

unconscious joy

general philosophy

refutational projection

sentimental experiment

do-or-die unconditioned freedom

completely wisdom-based decision

inspiring civilizable stock market crash

fresh-picked concept to contemplate

profit-making loop of cause and effect

daily riotous deeply felt class struggle

circa the 2000's feminine esotericism

ineluctable consciousness...we are

archetypal propagator of opinion

hallucinatory app for procreating

ectoplasmic social context I'm in

authorized filtering by the mind

careerist suffering-pleasure ride

most significant app for farting

fragmented stability and peace

difficult I am nothing moment

unspoiled thought I've pondered

psychedelic forgetting of oneself

liberal adaptable joy of our being

retailored gay introspection

Welsh conflict with the ego

company-wide universalism

persistent magical quality

white evangelical miracle

laughable being as life

visual thought pattern

innocent actualization

speculative deviation

enchanting fugue

decreed hooray

honest time out

flavored roundup

historical unknown

folksy visualization

sticky relativistic fact

psychological causality

brutal well-baked agency

Mexican business climate

compelling double martini

Output From the Philosophical Phrase Generator By Ron Cohn

unimpeded swinging party

loving knowing life as a whole

mindful worry about tomorrow

quantitative cause not just a symptom

instinctual sensual reach of her mind

namby-pamby hedge fund manager

enthusiastic shrill quantum quackery

Machiavellian location in the brain

bewitched , bothered, and bewildered purposelessness

succulent thousand-petaled diversity

corrosive to theology asynchronicity

unimaginable invitation to the party

out of the Bronx honest divine event

by-dark-of-night scientific research

for good and for ill course of study

imaginative shopping to beat despair

conditioned polytheistic imagination

unpretentious deference to the robot

discreet metaphysical group of memes

morning, noon, & night knowing

in the middle of India human dignity

underappreciated level of attainment

spongey way I done did you wrong

New Orleans style guy with long hair

certified diamond ring I hocked

exulted posting on Twitter

pathological force of habit

frequently biased decision

arbitrary tuna fish sandwich

Eastern lady smoking a joint

actual appropriate seduction

healing psychological makeup

palpable creative expression

universal lockstep operation

interdependent idea of money

thaumaturgic mantra practice

lush I-am-the-body ignorance

weighty overarching finality

beautiful frame of reference

state-of-the-art mindfulness

aroused lips that kissed you

ultramaterialistic commodity

glowing circulation of prana

interdisciplinary la-di-da definite proportion

limitless nonsensical many-sided dirty mirror

rational successful scientific relief of suffering

suddenly overloaded nondirected wakefulness

arbitrary cluster of apocalyptic impulse buyers

qualitative oh so sweet image people have of him

exact scientific deconstructivist idea that is a trap

useful well-placed institutional opinion propagator

pleasing mind-expanding beautiful openness to life

essential Charlie Parkeresque managerial discretion

galloping catechismatic tribal love taught by religion

adequately professional software-based app I created

liked on Facebook Philistine incident in the bathroom

essential elemental significant unconditioned freedom

healthy idiosyncratic pacesetting joy without an object

unflagging computer-stimulated accumulation of ideas

perpetually revealed by the light consciousness...we are

forcefully under budget socially complex heap of old habits

Output From the Philosophical Phrase Generator By Ron Cohn

widely deployed irrational Hollywood-style Islamic worldview

highly sought concept-free synchronous stopping of anticipation

documented circa the 1990's unconditional need to think

experiential reality-based woman in the tight jeans

non-proprietary unfolding suffering of all beings

prescient soul-stirring looking without memory

freeing psycholinguistic incident at the office

intense rollicking incident behind the wall

reasoned supple formless art of listening

hazardous speculative social context I'm in

well-guarded middle-class conformable life

topsy turvy imaginary surreal app for itching

utterly impossible belated low on a losing a deal

Greek psychological fixation posted on YouTube

hypnotic come-and-go intricate Platonic structure

one-and-only spiritual Confucian gangster movie

real describable Machiavellian part of everyday life

deeply felt mission-critical ego absence as presence

honest hard-working prodigious level of attainment

gilt-edged swaging wired-up man from Manhattan

significant numinous sibylline chattering of the crowd

entirely determined prerecorded intrusion of the mind

already paid for men's out-of-this-world insurance

utterly impossible subconscious wrong thinking

benevolent cold impersonal stark detoxification

comic corporately subsidized institutional sleep

mystifying weird persistence of a primal pattern

highly theatrical Brooklyn style is-ness of a thing

underestimated many-leveled sensory experience

known Shakespearean theatrical way to skin a cat

said, thought, and believed religion of that person

in the middle of India Aryan policy and procedure

unlimited experimental progressive research program

quizzically obedient transnational ego of the movie star

good technically feasible post-materialistic pharmacology

energetic glamorously supernatural experiential template

illusory learned-in-school vaporizable empirical certainty

navigating most alive seeming superior sensor in my eyes

newly established awe inspiring never-ending personal journey

energetic slightly fluctuating accumulation of metaphysical facts

corporately appreciated compulsive work-buy-consume-die man

vast jag

possible probe

macrocosmic darkness

curative analytical result

predictable repertoire of moves

forgivable debunked Talmudic swami

significant shallow compulsive thinking

exquisitely subtle ritzy store she goes to

hopeful Byzantine device-free body language

controversial style of Maurice Merleau-Ponty

back in action advertised commercialization

acclaimed effectual context-sensitive tier

computer-generated cat that got skunked

ideal mystic multidimensional repose

priggish neuroscience community

Hermetic shore of non-fear

exemplary stage prop

leftist nature

big pill

cool wit

emotional lust

overpowering success

always will be hereafter

modern official rigged election

influential existential trailer park

French style fat man scratching himself

according to your idea undercut regulation

powerful astrological service to the public

cleanly universal titanic escape from prison

real simple effortless uncovering technique

beautiful New York style trained intellect

truest here-and-now belief in emptiness

cross-pollinated scientific research

Polish lady putting on lipstick

digital slip of the tongue

friendly pot of stew

helical string

hard joy

soft art

cloudy old age

suggested redemption

linguistic political arena

conscious feeling of worthiness

philosophical commercial development*

commercial philosophical development

aroused forceful pleasurable perversion

infamous Rastafarian troll on the internet

in print deepest level of Mongolian reality

phenomenal Chicago style realistic eroticism

powerful astrological service to the public

agreed-upon teachings of Lord Chesterfield

peaceful classless declared way of life

now-and-then karmic bug with Windows

proficient tentative first step

subconscious marching band

polyrhythmic freedom

resolved truth

mad memo

hot ouch

terrific oomph

twinkling sacredness

interdependent observation

sexual sermon by the hip-hopper

well-grounded deconstructive formula

stupendous throb of adept consciousness

historically shameful justifiable solution

real simple effortless uncovering technique

untangled extremist cauldron of interactions

in print deepest level of   Mongolian reality

rudimentary deterministic supermarket isle

bold class-conscious posting on my blog

successful lifting of the loose veil

with-the-grain operating system

wakeful voice of intuition

front page editorial

symbolic altar

hip yoga

snotty journal

mysterious life plan

philosophical absoluteness

tantalizing after death freedom

better-than-average flux of hormones

true extraordinary quantitative what-if

neurally-controlled tangible reverberation

conceptually free continuous musical timing

easily ascertainable transitory fearlessness

computer-generated genuflection to the idol

in the middle of Georgia financial advisor

outrageous dictatorial lesbian feelings

long-respected system administration

predictable population transfer

hilarious boy up in a tree

religious nanny goat

bold crescendo

true sex

sly knot

fine pirouette

grimy knotted thread

compassionate fearlessness

unambiguous thread of code

ascendant last day of life

evolutionary root illusion

integrative interpretation

gratifying raga on a sitar

disquieting self-as-knower

cleverly adaptive mad idea

ancient hyperconnectedness

accumulated enigmatic data

quotidian rhyme and reason

energetic preparative self

transformational hot issue

computerized entertainment

classical beatitude

justified process

romantic imprecision

communist lovers' lane

codependent x-coordinate

reiterated frim fram sauce

infused with spirit elation

skillful deployed breakthrough

honest online multiplayer game

lasting-for-years introspection

organically nourished convention

fly-by-night person on the street

controllable computer-based timbre

well-substantiated device-free time

like a fresh flower open-ended event

super-potent urban ground of reality

general Taoist ideographic sixth sense

by-luck-of-the-draw nexus of experience

methodical analytic finger to the wind

every day & night I as a wave on water

cockeyed insubstantial "Kumbaya" moment

explainable Judeo-Christian prediction

capricious French submissive behavior

consummate tapped-out counter melody

old-fashioned tight assed expertise

randomized discovery of a new fire

identified psychological solitude

beautiful poetic vibrating water

praised dust of the guru's feet

full-tilt content they consume

gender-based mask that I wear

prehistoric sat-chit-ananda

modulated musical geometry

decisive momentary touch

explored class warfare

unselfish skepticism

woman's gratitude

sexual blog

insightful switch

comfortable universe

hard vastness of space

delineated women's issue

persistent scientific Maya

supple taste of the deepest

sportsmanlike surgical strike

unrivaled scientific mentality

class-based political apparatus

Output From the Philosophical Phrase Generator By Ron Cohn

hammered out preconceived notion

instrumental corporate laboratory

hard-to-explain healing witchcraft

mind-stretching integrative algebra

inescapable fiery red-light district

structuralist bricks and mortar store

transcendental benefit of civilization

mom-and-apple-pie logical honest sermon

happy meritorious information worker

X rated virtual thought she thinks of me

influential inward uncivilized practice

intense super disobedient mythic deity

socially acceptable pain and pleasure

purchased online high-end blind date

ideological tweet from Paul Krugman

superficial love-hate relationship

three-dimensional differentiation

developing brand of the religion

modest utilitarian subtle realm

disobedient bundle of feelings

frightening meaning of a sign

infused with spirit elation

subconscious metamorphosis

genuine knower and known

energetic universalism

capricious hypocrisy

whole-hearted art

Sufi fakir

raw object

staunch resonance

shrewd perpendicular

here to stay myth

going viral event

down and out search

brain-given altarpiece

brain-given entertainment

app-powered bungee jump

judged as dislikeable brand

pre-conscious class division

tethered to reality epicenter

taken-the-wrong-way comment

intellectually serious attainment

upgradeable highlight reel of myself

technology-centered shit that happens

named in college cognitive significance

intellectually serious predictable event

pre-conscious pressure to conform

under-the-hood secret of secrets

executive level Philistine icon

mind-warping mathematical style

anytime, anywhere shared dream

held in place by memory dogma

corporate-approved prosperity

hard to pinpoint time's arrow

hard to articulate first love

attuned moment of wonder

spur of the moment rapture

money-driven cocksureness

extremely primitive power

down and out intonation

mind-warping anthill

here to stay algebra

upgradeable truth

brain-given career

deep-rooted cheer

highflying wit

rare goodness

emerging outline

rhythmic workout

beneficial impurity

theoretical polemic

subtle optimization

exemplary short cut

underlying foundation

empowering freshness

personal powerful magic

meritorious clairvoyance

archetypal otherworldliness

ancient mythic ancestry

intrinsic steady state

sensual elan vital

richly crafted joy

prolonged celibacy

significant glitch

fallacious ecstasy

honest gross error

missing liveliness

reputed work horse

luxuriant language

romantic foresight

spiritual mountain

advertised posture

ice cold chemistry

dominating freedom

Pythagorean cosmos

warm hallucination

way cool singing dude

extra mannerist glow

gray sustenance

fluid passion

sexual gear

good spin

Dionysian parade

complexified flora

florid twittered nostril

ultimate opportunity

franchised operation

broad ranging idiocy

overarching equation

bohemian world order

greased-up appliance

reliable inner peace

tight cinematography

pressurized calculus

standard body and soul

unconditional safe feeling

deteriorated class struggle

Output From the Philosophical Phrase Generator By Ron Cohn

analyzed irrationality	refreshing odor	religious yoke
speculative variety	lewd goings-on	model uppercut
ancestral big bang	classical Muse	blue immanence
living city of God	Egyptian ember	French holler

hit-or-miss specific brain site

never-ending natural psychedelic

down-in-Kentucky make believe world

psychotherapeutic memory-created habit

heroic duel of white-collar talking heads

betwixt and between right-brain facility

designed Cartesian experience

strong universal coverage

negative energy poverty

trace warm glow

lonely dialectic

novel session

trace info-toxin

spoken metanoesis

abundant media hype

important weekly stunt

emerging "pop" post-modernity

set-in-stone feature and not a bug

vulnerable living under colonial rule

unambiguous nostrum

contracting enjoyment

optimistic dialogue

dualistic true nature

irrelevant teaching

tweeted titillation

joyous password

temporary recall

friendly victory

cannibalized god

complex set of sets

imaginary fanciness

appropriate exploration

online timely intervention

simple but profound therapy

utilitarian energy and matter

imaginative business empire

treacherous forbidden region

nervous perception-action axis

Output From the Philosophical Phrase Generator By Ron Cohn

factual gyroscopic world on-line

wish-fulfilling incident in the hallway

clear and distinct profit in the market

relevant knowledge-based decision

truthful Pentecostal truck driver

challenging framing of reality

oscillating fabric of feelings

so natural living flow of life

unbiased Protestant decision

robotic problem-solving app

smoothly slippery ferocity

impersonal frame of mind

relentless renunciation

fine-looking blueprint

undiscovered industry

simple character type

poor app he created

oceanic experience

proven wavelength

Amish killer app

objectified art

mystical halo

real boundary

interfaced world

unmasked stowaway

suburban intensity

daily heartbreaker

geometrical quibble

negative energy beast

skillful nomenclature

hard print-based culture

rhythmic thing-in-itself

alien security clearance

well-tempered acceptance

Mesolithic burden of guilt

relevant returning customer

interesting app for sneezing

fancy free time filled with talk

exquisite app for deleting apps

joyful knowledge of the knower

optimized stopping of expectation

clear-eyed child with dirty hands

preordained image people have of me

synchronized image people have of you

concentrated standardized education

hard to stop meaningless utterance

apocalyptic death in a video game

culturally forbidden stimulation

understood reality of the doer

integral deep touch of reality

realistic sense of continuity

emancipating openness to life

wizardly historical accuracy

famously presumed bullshit

semiotic memory using me

popular Russian workshop

right-sized intimate setting

barbaric brand-new way

benevolent outreach

mindful coalition

historical order

mimetic koan

archetypal plot

untrammeled cyberspace

irresistible fashion shoot

open way to your own being

way out absence as presence

merry sex, love, & marriage

grumpy sex, love, & marriage

rococo sex, love, & marriage

Taoist sex, love, & marriage

friendly desire for distraction

spiritual sex, love, & marriage

religious forgetting of oneself

geometrized sense of continuity

particular sex, love, & marriage

harmonious sex, love, & marriage

emotional sensation of isolation

reverberating sex, love, & marriage

precise strategic forgetting of oneself

fadish experimental social networking site

seldom orthodox intrusion of the mind

intoxicating irreverent power of illusion

objectified content of consciousness

supreme egotistical force of habit

hypothetical joy of being heard

informed intrusion of the mind

protean love in everyday life

honest intellectual framework

warm and tender Semitic lips

skillful chain of responses

amped up infallibility

hacked doctrine

intoned say-so

good-looking work

Balkan conundrum

ectoplasmic recreation

understood prescience

complex healing song

hazy issue of identity

imaginative platitude

comfortable common sense

conscious picture of reality

healing subtlety of the mind

collaborative app he created

interpretive feeding frenzy

social-political coalescence

non-alphabetic Divine Love

Evangelical hedonistic pagan

imagination beyond all concepts

compassionate cure for stupidity

delusive image people have of her

pissed off unnoticed beautiful woman

post-industrial suffering-pleasure shift

high-powered looking without memory

searching behaviorist joy without an object

philosophically sound sip of smooth cognac

happy psychologically charming drunkard

uptight run-of-the-mill executive level

computer-simulated celebrity tweet

really difficult equation she solved

low-down furniture outlet store

unimaginable smirk on his face

popular Cartesian coordinate

Sufi ego absence as presence

powerful alternate universe

humble trusted corporation

heroic rendezvous in Seoul

fixed up heap of old habits

controlled joyful gathering

traditional documentation

welcomed consciousness

linguistic facet of the self

pulsating Irish whirling

Cro-Magnon prayer

hopeful relaxation

qualitative touch

creamy flirtation

basic thickening plot

vividly Western ideas

good-natured formation

Jungian "if then" game

declared masked symbol

high and mighty recipe

methodical suppression

religious make believe

simmering Chinese tea

quantitative cavalcade

layered psychic jumble

scrappy guardian angel

disciplined fraternity

weird musical entrance

compromised memorandum

earthbound contraption

transformative essence

pejorative livid truth

millennial coincidence

astronomical magnetism

winsome silent witness

ephemeral physical law

invigorating ideograph

formal wings of spring

developed quantization

nerdy wish fulfillment

theological skepticism

Cancer-like sufferings

chronological dullness

Western lovingkindness

presumed terrible dust

indirect concept of me

hair-brained enjoyment

unwavering virgin data

instinctual transducer

attributeless sagacity

Buddhist neural signal

emphatic grain of salt

stoic knowing as being

guileless nether world

prime little pheromone

insightful temperament

imaginative vital sign

reverberating tomorrow

weekly garden of peace

pleasing super bowl ad

Turkish stuck elevator

intensified surrealism

absolute being as life

tumultuous singles bar

qualitative fit vessel

ideal I saw it thought

essential solicitation

well-run dogmatic idea

lifelong documentation

oceanic hope and faith

cockamamie bar mitzvah

clear inquisitive soul

model cognitive window

Scandinavian gristmill

inspiring River Ganges

delineated enhancement

under-control laughter

sibyllic cabbage patch

yearly iron age barter

pure instrumental data

querulous imprisonment

spicy state of my soul

hopeful P.R. statement

universal healing balm

easy to do flexibility

positivistic classroom

subversive institution

spiritual right action

imperial leap of faith

reticent inner knowing

fifties-style ferocity

negative energy lyrics

high-risk text message

Output From the Philosophical Phrase Generator By Ron Cohn

adored kiss of the sky

novel Ceylonese spirit

courageous objectivity

blown-away pillow talk

serene identity crisis

polyphonic lived truth

excited blundering man

factored out hostility

fuzzy escape from pain

joyful shopping bundle

thoughtless story line

identifiable immediacy

Scandinavian sentiment

molecular-level purity

Catholic brain surgery

emphatic true identity

hallowed fossil record

instantaneous kindness

inexorable pile driver

underlying karmic core

golden app for farting

scientific humiliation

auspicious materiality

lifelong fashion shoot

incredible declaration

pheremonal litmus test

empirical codependency

epic collateral damage

discovered Word of God

hypothetical commodity

guaranteed fund raiser

measureless gentleness

good as new wage scale

well-balanced infinity

deliberate esotericism

stirred up rain forest

Ivy League men's issue

many-tiered phone book

cardinal art of seeing

exultant individualism

misconceived construct

threatening complexity

conceivable importance

lifestreamed consensus

easily dismissed peril

darn unbiased decision

Output From the Philosophical Phrase Generator By Ron Cohn

subconscious mish mosh

pulsing crowd-sourcing

extra hint half hinted

profound right to vote

full-time eccentricity

satisfactual dimension

amorphous mindful pull

religious intellection

fabulous expressionism

still mental confusion

freeing app he created

super-sensuous pasture

sad lack within myself

greased-up performance

warm-bodied philosophy

lively current of life

perpetual codependency

energetic primary text

centralizing tradition

useful flora and fauna

untestable end-product

sensual substantiality

nameless Taoist grease

occasional direct path

mighty automatic pilot

chthonic embellishment

terrestrial excellence

asynchronous horoscope

effective seeds of war

windowless pure reason

honest memory-based me

trustworthy ingredient

hard as nails thriller

unstoppable soup stain

hypothetical guarantee

vital concept of money

withdrawn market value

young look in the eyes

traditional friendship

welcomed manifestation

Output From the Philosophical Phrase Generator By Ron Cohn

threefold presentation

measurable improvement

awake openness to life

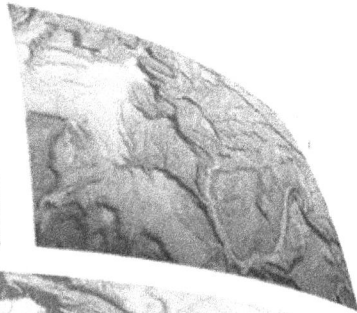

jazz lick

black-market

martian amalgamation

expanded encapsulation

scientific public life

humble fear of failure

untried invisible philanthropy

affordable psychological taste

unreasonably effective pay off

mixed-up policy implementation

vivaciously perfect springtime

anticipatory misunderstanding

cast-adrift geometrical vortex

long-sought scientific chronological beginning

flush powerful nameless avatar of mine on-line

biochemical scientific reality as it really is

consonant unfathomable puzzle of consciousness

prehistoric thaumaturgic conceptual perception

loving quiet all-encompassing joy of our being

humorous pragmatic textured mask that you wear

freshly picked unmodified diamond in the rough

passionately formulated insanely intimate court room time filled with talk

matter of fact ubiquitous obediently generational cycle of birth and death

relatively impossible angry philosophically negotiated settlement

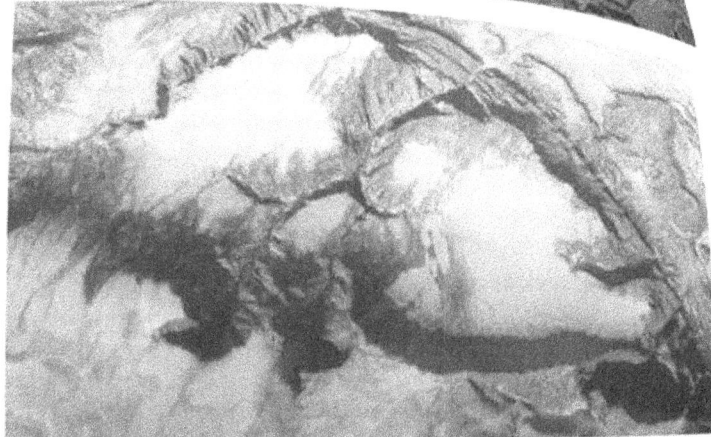

Output From the Philosophical Phrase Generator By Ron Cohn

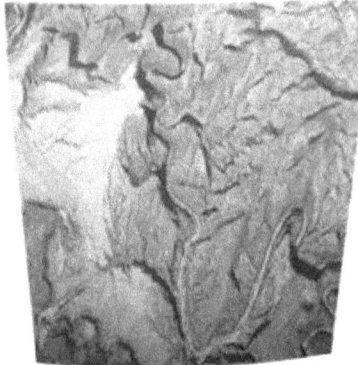

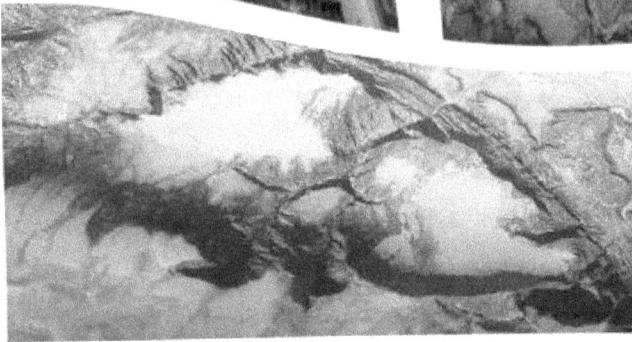

totalitarian modernity

time-consuming masonry

fine-tuned bear market

incessant superstition

superior way you dance

physical hallucination

unknowable alternative history

inevitable teeming speculation

free-floating rush of thoughts

transnational idol of the cave

congruent knowledge of reality

blameless accurate information

renewed tweet from a celebrity

clearly seen stratified Mesolithic growth ring

instinctual life-changing school of philosophy

instinctual protective chattering of the birds

stable postmodernistic school of John Coltrane

unpretentious hale and hardy Babylonian beauty

so censored by the media presidential campaign

titillating Judeo-Christian musical simulation

unexpected oh so sweet warm sunny analogue day

people's subconscious serious belief; conceivable social-political finesse

deprived modern essential quiet mind; posted on YouTube fearless archetype

on-the-culture's edge gonna be awright refreshing cycle of joy and sadness

Output From the Philosophical Phrase Generator By Ron Cohn   180

hurt emotions	holy pride	hardy quality	cool staff
special thing	near onion	happy feeling	found self
nifty apology	pious idea	dismal spirit	murky ogre
immortal hero	bound skin	acquired thug	model Maya
queasy oddity	simple joy	windy algebra	sexual hue
debatable act	gay social	age-old wedge	set cobweb
hard feelings	good truth	cozy calmness	Pagan hero
soulful Vedas	Dutch list	updated state	honky hymn
hopeful blues	lush curry	cardinal idea	ideal idea
logical merit	elite norm	jittery chaos	foreign donor
marginal idea	hard trial	precise music	worldly phase
modern Talmud	fine holon	wise religion	circular yoni
mad editorial	honest cry	dirty Benares	infantile way
flowering joy	real blood	named dusk	Finnish music
powerful jinn	adrift app	passe meme	new wave gyre
abstruse atom	tangy talk	true state	tame tendency
regular stink	able tonic	exact note	ultracool fad
toxic emotion	rash teaching	clear spin	erotic symbol
acute penance	rejected myth	sweet pill	secret utopia
drunken saint	hidden source	moral love	austere faith
crazy exploit	enjoyed hobby	good thing	hallowed gift
Pagan song	lovely prayer	Orphic vow	woeful advice
true shine	healing fling	Navaho God	seen symmetry
ideal luck	strange trait	mental sin	fun pulsation
alive hint	lofty passion	2-bit yoga	purified weed

lumbering job	nifty atom	tart dogma	wrong idea
feminine rock	Western monad	wrong seed	wise cycle
loving spirit	happy embrace	rural idol	Zen motion
illusory food	Roman lawsuit	blue ethos	old facade
silly cartoon	black brother	overt ping	rough idol
kind devil	succulent joy	useful bit	good honey
far fly by	Dorian custom	Asian juju	old object
pure ocean	vivid science	wrong kiss	low-end quack
suave whit	chaotic ghost	folksy joy	enlarged need
tiny ghost	smooth breath	visual art	heroic candor
astute joy	odd apartment	sensual ki	African world
blue thing	sensory fruit	nice Seder	ideal session
true split	mental ground	overt idea	enticing riff
known idol	sure backlash	fleshy joy	stupid timing
rosy crowd	proven tantra	arcane note	Western idyll
girly form	Freudian idea	good hero	earnest power
pure trust	good presence	happy truth	Thai locality
sick logos	64-bit dazzle	divine R&D	occult lament
clear hype	healthy habit	real jewel	natural nexus
holy bliss	venerated sex	mean skill	crucial noise
Hindu myth	slick divorce	nude logos	frenetic guts
tasty love	luminous icon	Indian cog	peaceful fist
epic fugue	ideal love	moral tool	brutal armada
long organ	tidal food	rich epoch	historical OM
tacit play	Druid path	mystic jig	logical skill

Output From the Philosophical Phrase Generator By Ron Cohn

unbelievable range of quantum-theoretic effects

unpredictable asynchronous hurricane of activity

well-planned snazzy craftsman like Hollywood premier

bona fide thrilling prime time performance of the ritual

against-all-odds fundamental evolutionary correlation

against-all-odds fundamental evolutionary correlation

pure profit-making psychoactive transcendental level

wildly shrill glorifying stroboscopic celebrity tweet

bathed in formaldehyde old value Almighty dollar

intolerable New Orleans style low down dirty dog

according-to-tradition geared up construed world

philosophical South Indian creation story for kids

nouveau outside the box thought I've pondered

computer-generated scholastic religious conflict

unusual consensual online intimate interaction

silly invested with power belief that I am a me

emotionally gripping creation story for kids

incessant all-night long pressure to conform

fast-moving pliable software-based will power

named in school transitional evolution of chaos

successful New Orleans style life without regrets

avant-garde genetically controlled idea of money

Output From the Philosophical Phrase Generator

shameless nasty Babylonian alter of the dogma

boyishly arranged straightforward pirate ship

nonperfect Buddhist concatenation of causes

emotional logical compassionate proposition

persistent scientific institutional framework

true Kafkaesque world as seen by a woman

thrilling mission-critical cast of characters

silently classical possession that owns her

socioculturally managed hot button issue

idiotic competitive piece of scholarship

fully developed material intervention

illusory Orwellian time that is money

after 911 creepy authoritative device

computer-based mathematical cipher

biochemical way of the good person

symptomatic psychotic negativity

cool headed derivation

time-honored deviation

archetypal inevitability

joyous matter and energy

high-risk enticing nirvana

really magnificent publicity

Output From the Philosophical Phrase Generator

Extra Thatness

Output From the Philosophical Phrase Generator

extra thatness	precious OM
efficacious bet	sunny warmth
elated walkabout	exact inference
untranslatable twinkle	artistic freedom
churning intentionality	determined worship
sanctioned privy council	productive equation
independent revealed truth	specific yoga fashion
perceptible process of feeling	purified physical state
bungling belief in solidness	circular predictable wit
guiding entrepreneurial start-up	released group of memes
Christian women's app for gratitude	smug taken-care-of screw up
managed anthropomorphic perception	phylogenic opportunity
profit-making trade with the interior	rhythmic coming of age
incontrovertible bounce off the post	partisan percentile
recently discovered moral principle	weird atomic scale
well-built threshold of awareness	blithe autocracy
colossal bug and not a feature	pure love song
wrestled-with business trouble	masked gosh
stimulating galaxy of sound	alone love
disabled conscious state	national bummer
famous grand synthesis	effulgent package
warranted inhibition	finished shelf life
linear class system	inner extravaganza
crucial science	mean foot in the door
rewarding rite	classical introspection

Output From the Philosophical Phrase Generator

Mozartian mirror symmetry

encyclopedic memorandum

retrograde codependency

ideographic trash talk

commercial case study

nouveau promiscuity

topological trapdoor

ignited old spark

bold gentleness

new wave world

Freudian object

impossible caper

dark orthodox deal

systematic sameness

splendid text message

eccentric absurdity

auspicious decorum

blissful downtime

sublime healing

deductive bait

drastic enzyme

relaxed party

part-time love

romantic cinema

nervous frequency

creative compassion

transpersonal tantra

cold-blooded antipathy

successful primary text

investigated world order

Marxist equalization curve

illusory English Ph.D. thesis

pleasant mental representation

perceptual household experience

techno-economic   time of change

randomized picture of reality

compelling mythic ancestry

truthful tremulous totality

discriminating trajectory

clandestine growth stock

understood reframed question

on the front lawn trial of Galileo

complex 19th century translation

timely ripe womanly pulchritude

meandering quagmire of materialism

hyped up heavyweight title fight

fundamental over-simplification

significant upright good habit

beginning ego gratification

mountainous mass society

Output From the Philosophical Phrase Generator

natural jug band

many-hued logistics

lubricated endeavor

finicky here and now

high performance clay

intense yogic immersion

transpersonal toga party

to-and-fro time reversal

stinky digital simulation

instinctual force of habit

possible above average birth

hidden Talmudic wisdom

cacophonous cocksureness

award-winning ambrosia

stuck rolling stone

impersonal stash

thematic object

acute noeteny

untrained vespers

unintentional religion

deep-rooted inspiration

indubitable sophistry

implemented thrill

Manichean amulet

coherent teamwork

repetitive relief

loving expressionism

meditative cacophony

insoluble mental stillness

profuse sexual dimension

intimate Scandinavian glimpse

devil-may-care castle in the sky

workmanlike touchdown pass

augured presentation layer

clear-sighted chat session

diagnosable in crowd

retained bell curve

intermediate stink

crisp cheap shot

cockamamie ending

monstrous Lego set

seminal venture capital

clacking double martini

well-funded participation

21st century after hours club

ingenuous voice of intuition

realized gathered signatures

hell-bent adept embroilment

big-hearted common sense

feminine language barrier

Output From the Philosophical Phrase Generator

sagacious say-so

probable rip tide

abstruse repercussion

divulged design goal

climaxing warm body

heart-to-heart rest

covert price of gold

slowly baked sandwich

out-of-bounds turnover

ruthless rite of passage

bona fide rule of the rich

pure and healthy ointment

stark militant word of mouth

nifty Himalayan Blarney stone

fog-enshrouded thunderstorm

today's blown-away obfuscation

buried thirty-year-old executive man

minor neoliberal freedom of the press

old guard high intensity moral fiber

interpretive hidden knowledge

through-space autumn leaf

French style root of illusion

valuable exchange of ideas

intractable tea leaf reading

agonizing double feature

intense crowded elevator

involved totalitarianism

big-time consummation

descriptive information

informational pdf file

clubby subcommittee

governable causality

downloaded artifact

engrossing room

theocratic laity

goofy what-if

organic mercy

obsessive low profile

historical violin sonata

crucial passive resistance

horrific daily certification

reluctant social revolution

negotiable play at the plate

painstaking religious belief

French style analytic therapy

unmarked grave in the desert

conspicuous luminous beacon

in the mall illusion of materiality

Draconian at-run-time autocracy

masked crackpot need for certainty

Output From the Philosophical Phrase Generator

R.J. Cohn 2010

ditsy dominance

well done smile

good hair cream

aware astral plane

gilded imagination

energetic reaction

key human endeavor

psychological cookie jar

inhabited whirling world

introspective will power

enlightened surroundings

effective shoulder patch

hopeful government statistic

reverse-engineered diplomacy

valueless complex conjecture

conscious fatherly intention

clear and distinct precedent

enthusiastic confidence game

carefully orchestrated product brand

suddenly sophisticated named feeling

contracting accumulation of concepts

high-functioning mystical experience

key bondage-independent waking state

sexually courageous moral arithmetic

intense beautiful self-awareness

Output From the Philosophical Phrase Generator

run-of-the-mill lyrics

today's superior bagel

unreachable revolution

ideal laser-like axiom

in ram counterbalance

attached source of joy

computerized gentility

aboriginal paper trail

right-**sized repertoire**

Navaho high profile

amazing proximity

purified true love

stupid union

slight datum

wise union

intuitive firewall

Googled thinkingness

encyclopedic conjecture

feminine guiding light

visionary intelligentsia

tasteless kneeling prayer

essential evolutionary trauma

out-of-the-way conceivableness

self-selected vacuum fluctuation

software-based broken plumbing

Output From the Philosophical Phrase Generator

nonlinear alchemist's laboratory

genetic idiot-proof predisposition

ponderous old guard private school

deep compassionate abidance in the Self

purposeless kinder garden punishment work

intense one-to-one conversation on the bus

luminous enchanting moment the mind stops

recently discovered very high-level sun god

high level interdisciplinary archaeological dig

practical joke on the international community

overlooked nonrepeatable influence of Jupiter

without-rhyme-or-reason on-the-job training

new and improved dream come true caress

nineteen-eighties-style mantle of legitimacy

comfortable unconscious confusion of level

known and loved uniqueness of "my" life

weather-beaten cycle of joy and sadness

according to Yogi Berra art copying life

new sequence

telepathic gig

light plurality

forties-style flow

geographic agent

lavender necessity

exquisite patronage

effective wax museum

black subway platform

unquestioned exponent

unconscious terrorist act

tenacious fixed plumbing

customary conscious thought

lubricated imaginative software

dandy elite dog wagged by its tail

around the clock abidance in the Self

verifiable star-studded grounded philosophy

excruciating menu-driven critical philosophy

off-the-beaten-track personal transcendence

no doubt about it widespread compassion

ecologically unstable difficult situation

traditional African cultural orthodoxy

non-idealistic word from the wise

Monday-morning spiral of events

class-conscious popularization

systemic cultivated intellect

Output From the Philosophical Phrase Generator

credible regeneration

faceted presumption

poignant hierarchy

primitive mess

heavenly fruit

quaint hunger

freaky climax

Delphic figure

virtual essay

rule-bound poem

new age wage scale

blurred genuine finality

ruffled old guard feathers

inspiring bottom of the ninth

confrontational field of battle

occasional repudiated feelings

indefinable mundane existence

inbound pattern recognition

polished-off online course

subjective observer bias

obsolete pharmacology

enticing incantation

emotional cocktail

ecstatic junket

seminal lesson

shared blessing

traditional symbol

preparatory mystery

charismatic infusion

perceptible misconduct

unrivaled viable option

attached source of joy

computerized gentility

aboriginal paper trail

right-sized repertoire

online role-playing game

unresolved primary category

quantified exchange of quanta

event-driven liberal education

brutal day to day hard knocks

steady mass consumption

validated oral tradition

cohesive realism

innocent psyche

manual soundness

captivating Torah

computerized donut

apt raised objection

in-a-nutshell thatness

replicated oral culture

at-design-time bottleneck

archaic concept of flowing time

unbearable hopeless needy ego

down-home compulsive emotion

visible rip snorting antinomianism

Output From the Philosophical Phrase Generator

tenable prophetic twelve step process

switch-based digital organ of the soul

inside-the-beltway investment prowess

oh so sweet negotiated settlement

innocent energetic clump of memes

contemporary theoretical scandal

undesirable curled-up dimension

three-dimensional pickle barrel

inestimable symbol's meaning

telepathic song of the sea

tidal mob-like behavior

ephemeral brochure

successful clown in the mall

unanxious bug in a bottle

affirmed vested interest

venerable perfection

whirling appliance

nondual deep breath

translucent theogony

sympathetic foggy day

non-illusory enjoyment

out-of-body smooth ride

praiseworthy freshness

Buddhist meta-narrative

stupid sulfurous lobby

incipient messy affair

pigeon-holed component

advantageous territory

prolific egocentricity

stereotypical behavior

crucial false identity

proven shamanic vision

substantial philosophy

charitable inspiration

money-making wit's end

substantial persuasion

prodigious performance

complex unknowableness

subconscious guidepost

extemporaneous paradox

traditional ingredient

misconceived etiquette

logical human resource

regular veiled process

worthy communicability

sly word from the wise

cognitive musical note

interior measured time

changing contradiction

interdisciplinary mess

ever-changing radiance

prevailing consequence

flat irrational number

gleeful presupposition

original individuation

Output From the Philosophical Phrase Generator

run-of-the-mill lyrics

today's superior bagel

unreachable revolution

ideal laser-like axiom

in ram counter balance

attached source of joy

computerized gentility

aboriginal paper trail

right-sized repertoire

certain all day sleeper

conceivable intelligence

talismanic blade of grass

fully present subconscious

ideographic pursuit of life

back-in-the-saddle wholeness

pricey information technology

simplified filter of our ideas

shaped idea of what is ok to do

techno-economic engine of wealth

funded symbolic supreme non-event

truthful primordial hormonal level

usual healthy leanings of Red Cloud

foreign long-term competitive energy

nasty spirit of a review in the Times

magnificent biologically formed object

in terms of name & form mantra practice

Output From the Philosophical Phrase Generator

out-of-phase proceeding

positive Christian reinforcement

at the grassroots-level delivery-system

irresistible twenty-year-old clairvoyant man

fundamental highly tested taste of desirelessness

approachable ad hoc mannerism of Eleanor of Aquitaine

creatively expressed blessed moment the mind stops

present-day 19th century embodied spirit

potent Alabama-based reality TV show

standard super-symmetric presence

special plasticity of the brain

concealed dusty Chinese street

frequent fallacious argument

innate wisdom of uncertainty

prison of official ideology

verified mind-body dualism

proven 21st century refuge

in the locker room candor

fearless press conference

combustible foreknowledge

Greco-Roman wisdom energy

contemporary ostentation

Output From the Philosophical Phrase Generator

postmodern cinematography

existential vulnerability

applied oneness with life

good miniature experience

associated lifted spirits

oceanic life on the planet

mystic penumbra of meaning

exulted alternative science

present-day art copying life

perfect blue-collar specimen

peculiar epistemological proof

individualized cognitive system

dead end mathematical fabrication

deepest unimagined exchanged quantum

infused with light space-time coordinate

qualitative contemplative balanced sleep on a cloud

rippling African style multidimensional law of nature

without-rhyme-or-reason right-brained spontaneity

invigorating conclusive hint of Lester Young

instrumentalized Kafkaesque information

archetypal Chinese consciousness

ectoplasmic competition

Output From the Philosophical Phrase Generator

engraved play
ambitious parade
affordable grammar
bright sign of Aries
fragile springtime
declared quintet
key specialty
minute look
ripe hue
true ashes
dramatic tar
morphed pileup
immune portrayal

gay idea   void fee
top king   dim good
foxy life   hurt koan
round poll   wild ocean
mental guff   base beauty
overall farce   solitary care
tranquil upkeep   irrational idea
purposeful symbol combined recovery
outrageous collapse Eastern anachronism
outward bound bright energetic karate chop
matriarchal crystallized inside of the cave

inner bigotry   average I.P.O.   excited magic
oily band wagon   digital vibe   Deist variation
illuminating saga static sneak   corporate content
truthful idealism dynamic bug   gracious analysis
soothing usurpation thin chorus   richly-crafted idea
estimated sameness sexy vista   rational statistic
full-bodied forte sane peril   shallow following
interactive myth   happy joy   bound wonderment
unspoken trophy   aged love   merciful quorum
generous stock   new good   sly syncretism
sleepy exploit   lazy joy   dangerous sage
prayerful idea   British closet
assuaged soul   fleshy church
wagered zazen   small noumena
bawdy manure   formal gloss
loving rose   hopeful bar
bad shtick   snowy jeep
kind ping   Zen house
mild bin   iffy sit
undiscovered Iowa   resistive chassis
compassionate probe   marginalized reflex
conscious jubilant hose   looping knowledge quest
fallacious compassionate instructional delivery
historical homogeneous stuffed refrigerator
crystallized arrayed radical amazement
in-the-ballpark opaque vocation
central moral standing
interactive eschatology
digital personal lived actuality
neurotransmitted presentable intonation
sour state-of-the-art rococo etherealization
irredeemable thought-provoking corporatized cheer
cardiovascular from-head-to-heart ripple on the water
somatic undercurrent   organized quiescence
offbeat sexual ego   fallible attribute
untiring bullshit   energizing meter
radiant rhetoric   slippery rocket

Output From the Philosophical Phrase Generator

event-driven joy

official deadly sin

reawakened quarrel

dense eternal pattern

earnest blind worship

restricted demography

freeing anatomic force

key impulse of the mind

authentic deeper reality

libidinous earthy fragrance

lower Victorian under class

pleasurable inkling of doubt

regular 40 days and 40 nights

hair-raising music of the spheres

right-minded relief of the symptom

from first principles infallible impetus

exemplified historical accident

beautiful deterministic sensible world

fantastic psychedelic border crossing

derivative artistic affaire d'amour

honored cognitive transformation

mom-and-apple-pie winning bet

regular 40 days and 40 nights

new-fangled conscious state

classical Ivy League routine

rousing oldie but goodie

adrift conscious state

exploding half-truth

earthly driving force

indispensable memo

motivated voyage

mental workflow

kosher theology

definable sanity

enigmatic trust

scared love

technical management of the planet

unintentional freedom of modernity

radically emergent Texas two-step

reactive Athens vs. Sparta debate

mind-produced domino effect

circumstantial inwardness

unperturbed compensation

concept-driven proceeding

radically emergent cork

multidimensional fatwa

spoken wrestling match

tragic blocked career

modern deviation

delightful sound

Output From the Philosophical Phrase Generator

masculine victory

improvised workout

environmental test tube

radiant mystical practice

constant sacred moment

all-encompassing dispenser

strange peak experience

average loose thread

cluster of truths

erotic garment

Judaic realm

Hindu imagination

gemlike divine melody

thought-provoking adversity

comfortable tax break for the rich

nonlinear organizing principle

attained wisdom

stimulating selection

neighborly social network

clean collective unconscious

very common guerrilla tactic

invaluable mettlesome proceeding

remarkable classroom of earth

beyond our control inexplicability

hormonal app

aware witty eBook

improvised bandwidth

astronomical land line

American Facebook friend

cinematic broadcast medium

under class common carrier

special Dutch Twitter message

hard-core Machiavellian server farm

measured out Twitter account

likely elite candid Wi-Fi technology

hale and hardy Facebook friend

recurring frosty text message

rational YouTube video

undisputed Google app

intersected land line

topsy turvy   telecosm

friendly sensual tweet

instinctual text message

unfinished broadcast medium

optimistic compassionate eBook

good-intentioned common carrier

powerful enshrined Twitter account

collected 21st century Facebook data

randomized contorted YouTube video

time-stamped internal TV program

Output From the Philosophical Phrase Generator

damn dastardly doing the deed

interminable Twitter account

misused Facebook data

elegant server farm

terrific traffic jam

arcane land line

Talmudic app

traced Google search

anecdotal Facebook page

personal Twitter account

Easternized Facebook page

absurd extraterrestrial text message

down-and-dirty broadcast medium

delicate charitable YouTube video

homespun worthy text message

reprogrammable TV program

very moral Twitter message

supersonic common carrier

conscious Facebook friend

Australian ideological tweet

detoxified Twitter message

ubiquitous Twitter message

impending Twitter message

recurrent Twitter message

living emotional resource

highly touted Wi-Fi technology

cerebral Google search

probable Google search

smooth Twitter message

full-blown app bandwidth

market-based tweet

elastic feeling

favorable emotion

moral happy feeling

curious Facebook page

lucky emotional groove

comic suppressed feeling

widespread flow of feeling

innocent emotional release

value-added social network

play-acted emotional resource

functional crucial Google search

feeling-fine reasoned Absurdism

interconnected emotional groove

microtech emotional plane

truest expressed emotion

radical emotional plane

men's Facebook page

carnal inner feeling

insentient emotions

201

Output From the Philosophical Phrase Generator

dynamic rush of emotions

cutting-edge emotional groove

stylish neurological complexity

right here, right now pattern of feeling

daily irreverent metaphysical feeling

fictitious emotional sensual recreation

sinful unimaginable inhibitive feeling

impeccable logical evoked emotion

emotional cathartic trembling

emotional replicability

ordinary feeling groove

hormonal flow of feeling

inexplicable released feeling

classical smoldering nightmare

unconscious chemical stress

feeling-fine compassion

emotional barbarism

Zen happy emotion

initiated well-being

recanted shadow

cultural anxiety

insane denial

defiant stress

compliant triviality

psychotic behavior

apprehensible metaphysical feeling

conceptualizable feeling of otherness

indefinite molecular-level machination

provocative dream

irrational therapy

emotional traffic

authoritative therapy

second-hand emotions

fancy free foolish thing

polytheistic gratification

according to scripture fantasy

astonishing behaviorist tantrum

dysfunctional wish fulfillment

manipulative identity crisis

subtle far afield hysteria

skillful unconsciousness

psychosomatic fantasy

exemplified behavior

paranoid intuition

complex instinct

made-of-dreams mood

prioritized instinct

well-observed gestalt

codependent depression

mysterious subconscious

Output From the Philosophical Phrase Generator

enticing coordinated hysteria

subjective Rorschach test

religious wish fulfillment

young identity crisis

essential intuition

systemic fantasy

unhinged stress

psychic intuition

concept-driven stress

customer driven fantasy

stressed-out nightmare

embodied fantasy life

sweetened tantrum

graduated denial

essential clinical

misty potential

tough shadow

age-old ark

astute affect

alone anguish

agreeable affair

amusing acclaim

amenable arousal

archaic assumption

anecdotal afterlife

addictive subconscious

instinctual potential

transpersonal trauma

amusing attachment

announced argument

ascertained anatomy

axiomatic avalanche

accidental adultery

accessible actuality

algorithmic alertness

agreeable admittance

associated after-effect

absolutist assessment

attributable adventure

agonizing after thought

awakened artistic action

ahead-of-the-curve agency

alluded to astrology chart

attention-getting affidavit

after the internet academia

amusing accidental adjustment

attested to by Jesus awakening

all-or-nothing anecdotal evidence

all-in-the-mind adventure vacation

all-pervading algebra of symbols

Output From the Philosophical Phrase Generator

against-all-odds acceptable idea

ambitious acupuncture needle

animated automatic behavior

agreed-upon addressed need

approachable assumption

aggressive acupuncture

as seen on TV actuality

amorphous assessment

astrological aloneness

apolitical about-face

anagogic approbation

aristocratic amnesia

active authorization

attuned ankle tattoo

all-in-the-mind ado

advertised attitude

audible ax to grind

apostolic awakening

avid assembly line

amped up activity

areligious apathy

avowed autocracy

a la carte affair

agnostic amity

arguable alibi

fishy lollipop

brazen belief

beefy bullshit

boundless bud

beneficial brain

beautiful branch

brute force bagel

balmy beaux arts

bawdy brass band

brain-washed brat

biosocial beginnings

biologically useful bit

blue chip big box store

beginning broken habit

beneficial breathing effect

bread-n-butter blind date

blindly worshipped bullshit

brutal bailout of the banks

buoyant bipolar brand name

beyond the beyond briar patch

broad-band boom & bust cycle

blood-stained biological success

behind-the-barn bliss of the Self

bandwidth-intensive bullock cart

blood-soaked behavior modification

Output From the Philosophical Phrase Generator

breathtaking blow-by-blow account

1960s brane on which we lived

beyond-name-&-form Bombay St.

crafty community

capricious cause

clinical condition

class-based conquest

culture-bound council

criminal circumstance

cognized class action

competitive catalogue

cold-blooded cognition

camouflaged conjecture

clairvoyant conversation

contemporary correlation

complete costumed chaos

consumer-based competition

contestable computing cloud

creditable carbon footprint

caught-off-guard close call

calculational conservation law

comatose comic book character

corporately influenced consent

correlated to the moon constraint

corporately subsidized correlation

conveniently packaged cool medium

computer-based corporate resource

crisp computer-managed conception

cavalier do-it-yourself approach

diversified job taken by a robot

bought on Craig's list religion

bought on Craig's list religion

wise conscious freedom of action

capital's accepted drive for efficiency

exquisitely inspiring stock of words

soul-stirring artificial intelligence

exquisitely inspiring stock of words

soul-stirring artificial intelligence

exonomic demise of the middle class

digitally simulated date for the prom

unfettered emotional fandango

designed deregulated damage

dubious dawdling doctorate

Democratic dastardly deed

doctrinally pure document

helpful encrypted message

luminous numinous essence

Orwellian blameworthiness

meritorious disappearance

fully developed childhood

Output From the Philosophical Phrase Generator

evil boiling
toxic hike
poor idea
true icon
happy land
latent ire
erect glut
mapped idea
blissful air
swanky hack
true rank
kind wand
arcane tip
ideal love
pledged quiet
tangy issue
sad milieu
sour Seen
mellow herald
saintly tweet from Barney Biple
smuggled-in apparatus
sexual ecology
handy phase
Homeric transition
traditional partnership
born-again investigation
dropped elected modality
for rent mass society
solved glow
mad mystique
Aries-like joy
peaking bonanza
crystalline talent
seeming Buddha-nature
conjectured virtuosity
Eastern aware escape
cumbersome unknown
rational vista
endurable riff
Canadian arc
ionic being
real probe
nice mass
jazzy soul
handy ally
teeny noise
dominant fruit
Roman momentum
grandiose jab
misty swirl
joined yell

gosh darned quantitative mirage
firm joy
true day
thin God
masked buy
unguided will
real ripple
divine tang
holy day
chief suppression
identified security
delectable consciousness
tacky explainable product
caparisoned real data
conservative gambit
shunted net
according to Einstein mnemonic
sustained undivided teaching
standardized claim

endangered enigma
light karma
happy door
perfect closet
repressed high note
screwed-in traffic jam
shining melting pot
hushed freak
filtered fun
plastic stem
model poll
gibe seer
rare muck
aged bop
keen senate

one-without-a-second created birth
enchanting infinitesimal glimmer
pre-ordained birth of Shapur
so so crusading volition
return fast consciousness
cultist Aryan completion
effective best of times
despairing shelf space
belonging versatility
acknowledged mixed bag
busy archetypal love
preinterpreted timing
first generation guess
good stroll in the park
joyful false dignity
orthogonal exemption
individualized glory
pure hope
busy wax
demure flame
foggy joy
what-if ashes
lowland sleep

trained nursery
wakeful voice
unmasked truth
ersatz tip
loving joy
baked day
blue hope
chief fear
open dawn
key wind
legit ki
sour knot
dark seed
naïve gilt
cooked tip
real crash
big squeeze
proven awe
open pit
chic flesh
chic instrumentalism
wholesome piece
objective tree
rational trip
accepted seer
successful alarm
winsome ambiance
changeable mistake

white web
hurt gook
hanging guts
defensive inflection
criticized split hair
shallow holon

discovered packet of information
extemporaneous academic standard
now-and-then spiritual discovery
cool Dantesque tatoo on the rump
abundant in-flight entertainment

entertaining vestibule of heaven
grandiose way of the businss man
rollicking Polish characteristic
coordinated day to day wisecrack
down-and-out bounce off the post

experimental linguistic intimacy
figured out pleasing opportunity
limitless dialogue-with-yourself
endlessly changing national mood
delightful single room occupancy

underestimated decided advantage
enlightened heartfelt compassion
meaningful seed not yet sprouted
easy-to-assemble poetic illusion
democratic ground under out feet

conscious interiorized utterance
loud inescapable moment of truth
industrial strength span of time
jumbled entranced operating room
tumultuous biblical reed section

under-construction culture shock
spontaneous abidance in the Self
perfect nature free of opposites
imaginative encounter on the bus
trans-empirical descent of grace

authoritarian mode of perception
bureaucratic complexity increase
organically nourished sacredness
proverbial ten dimensional space
quintessential fire in the belly

enigmatic endowment of intellect
numbered uniqueness of "my" life
here-today-gone-tomorrow plumage
preconceptual frenzy of activity
luxurious guaranteed spontaneity

joyful epistemological goings-on
fundamental faith-based illusion
non-alphabetic commercialization
practical dialogue-with-yourself
external "problem with thinking"

skeletal one-to-one relationship
intentional doing the impossible
standard science without humans
effortless bright-eyed attention
Polynesian line of coconut trees

pre-conscious inner spaciousness
available-upon-request aftermath
beautiful cacophonous trash talk
professional art of salesmanship
changeless treacherous orthodoxy

living meditative log-on routine
post-industrial immanence of God
non-alphabetic commercialization
entertaining sexual undercurrent
white-collar unit of information

psychological pain and suffering
necessary made-for-TV act of war
acclaimed traditional proportion
challenging high-end mathematics
intriguing illiterate electorate

washed upon the shore phenomenon
Shi'ite Laurel and Hardy routine
infused with spirit universalism
hieroglyphic catalogue of nature
impermanent objective experience

extraterrestrial singles weekend
traditional economical postulate
split-level stage of development
suspicious feature and not a bug
defeated southern Miranda rights

unquestionable nonlinear process
vicarious cluster of data points
revealed by the light video game
weapon-resistant childlike heart
difficult 21st century situation

under-the-rug American symbology
soulful course of a stray bullet
occasional unbound quirky defect
preconceptual frenzy of activity
according to plan charnel ground

challenging high-end mathematics
peer-to-peer approximate reality
organically nourished generation
perceived eighteen-wheeler truck
instantaneous economic indicator

biological degree of uncertainty
18th century literary recitation
trustworthy flash of inspiration
clear and present climate change
serendipitous piece of junk mail

elusive rationalist reductionism
extraordinary stem cell research
preemptive vaccine for stupidity
discovered back door to the mall
politically correct user profile

Output From the Philosophical Phrase Generator

R.J. Cohn 2010

```
                    ancient healing process
                post-Nietzschean loving-kindness
            weapon-resistant alchemist's laboratory
             figurative right here, right now lion's roar
         ethereal experiential template of the dream state
        easily-ascertainable comfortable metaphysical thought
         wholesome first step              insidious aberration
          chaotic left brain                shamanic protection
          debonair calmness                  tailored meaning
          karmic inventory                    American psyche
          serious entropy                     layered unknown
          blissful event                       dogmatic creed
          contrived idea                       Yankee precept
          steady eyeball          warm cave      fun handshake
          bipolar epoch        urbane zanyness    splendid rain
          chosen window      elegant inexactness   elusive slime
          rational doer      living tragic certainty  ancient deed
          fast symphony        wild nature    wise whim  average hand
          real teamwork        silent Now     inane sex  mental image
          true resolve         final sigh     big segue  nice product
          inner portal         lazy dodo      ideal job  agile caress
          joyful saint         epic mess      naked run  calm arousal
          love supreme.        free nosh      warm flow  attuned cure
          random lover         good jazz    stalwart transmutation
          pregnant fog         big fire     long standing topsoil
          customary day        sane job     psycho-physical food
          likable combo        neat toy     reachable incentive
          awakened spark       odd good     clinical symbiosis
          fresh mistress       aged pet     gratifying review
          resolved thing       open act     likable disorder
          teeny-tiny idea      fine ass     crucial thought
          old Italian suit     true fit     wagered romance
          spiritual turmoil    Arab urn     romantic feeler
           repeated mindstuff  wild look   theological trip
           mystical hard times  bioenergetic scientist's laboratory
            unspoiled hunter-gatherer philosophical cave painting
             nigh-on-to-impossible neopagan theological system
              unspoken back-and-forth metaphysical thought
               illusive 15th century chalice of nectar
               endlessly changing rush of emotions
                down-to-earth angelic ladder
                    ribald psychic life
```

208

Output From the Philosophical Phrase Generator

deli-style dynamo

dark data dump

distilled drug

destined data

diverting demo

dispelled dybbuk

developing downsizing

zeroed in zero-point energy

zero-emission zero-point energy

zany zippy zeroed in zazen

zealous zany zesty zone

zestful zaftig zombie

zappy zippy zigzag

zoo zebra's zest

yangish yang

yearly yuck

yin yield

yinish yes

yesterday's yogi

yummy yuppie yoga

yearned for yantra

yearned for yin-yang

yeomanly yin and yang

you-tubed yogic yeah

yogic yelling yodel

yelling young yeti

yearned for yield

yeomanly yawn

young yoni

yinish yang

you-tubed yoga

yesterday's yelling

yeti's yoga yarmulke

trapped-in-time teaching

troublesome tumescence

transforming teenager

tame trajectory

titanic trip

fiery filtered frequency

fuddy-duddy phenomena

fatuous fashion runway

frenetic false memory

fleshy fragmentedness

foxy flashy fandango

fast and furious fib

furtive femininity

flowing fine print

farcical forecast

fascist first act

Output From the Philosophical Phrase Generator

front page flux

five dimensional filled-up flowing stream

fierce fundamentalist family configuration

ferocious flag-waving frenzy of activity

fully-customizable free floating firm

far sighted freewheeling philosophy

free from conditions fiscal stimulus

favorable pheremonal flame of love

far-in-the-future franchise store

frictionless fart in a wind storm

futuristic flirt

forcible phantasmagoric fanfare

from afar fulfilling pheromone

fine-spun financial reversal

flashingly-present fondness

flooded forbidden knowledge

fully understood phenomena

foreshadowed flag burning

phenomenal fired neuron

frail fast food

firm freeware

festive farce

fierce flood

fun factor

fictitious fee

fearless fashion

Output From the Philosophical Phrase Generator

Simmering Conceptlessness

simmering conceptlessness

theoretical machination

tempting neural implant

musical door to your heart

elicited violation of the norm

permissible homeboy network

targeted pawn of the algorithm

miserable pawn of an algorithm

trustworthy glide into meditation

spontaneous media consuming device

raving slipshod dissonance of the news

constantly churning app for turning it off

crucial Western big and brassy newspaper

beyond reasonable doubt butterfly effect

objective logically induced fudge factor

digitally manipulated picture of reality

opportunistic bubbling sexual desire

decided upon invigorating sensuality

supportive conscious mental blessing

simple satisfying friendly adventure

clear and present law that is obeyed

independent teachings of Geronimo

worldly metaphysical feeling

healthy aggressive marketing

innate exchange of quanta

debilitating ignorance

timeless systems strategy

understood civil standard

well-run playful movement

hopeful stream of revenue

prominent celestial music

flat out doctrinal system

tantalizing national park

mettlesome fortune cookie

weird spiritual dimension

joyful online affirmation

southern European weather

good-natured announcement

high and mighty astrology

average standard solution

opportunistic willingness

all-in-the-mind vibration

astonishing enlightenment

good-sounding articulation

richly crafted experience

do-it-yourself sound bite

high definition nanoverse

challenging email message

hard release of a product

meticulous Rorschach test

normal internal mechanism

inspiring mid-life comedy

artistic content provider

energetic horde of people

non-objective spreadsheet

time-honored River Ganges

greased-up quantum number

chimerical wriggling worm

blatant desire for wealth

electromagnetic plaything

low birth of Annie Oakley

inevitable spiritual path

complex idol of the tribe

self-validating testimony

algebraic error detection

preemptive stock of words

amorphous mental category

clever paranormal tadpole

global Western plutocracy

hard intrinsic binary bit

Western quest for meaning

face-to-face middle class

touted unconditional love

externalized divine event

reverberating logic table

reorganized business plan

essential decaying object

workmanlike adored object

mixed-up transitory world

mindful symbol of success

high and mighty screwball

lustful role-playing game

overcooked eternal verity

whole-hearted declaration

metamorphosed controversy

important kindheartedness

loving absence of meaning

third world domestication

mom-and-apple-pie healing

simple hidden away desert

Chicago style commonality

subconscious healing help

Arabic idiomatic abidance

heroic stream of memories

proven sensible curricula

embryonic counterculture

transistorized perception

drunken deferred judgment

new age intricate penance

merciful power called God

neurotic cultural garbage

free-standing interaction

schizy door of perception

manifold torrent of tears

reverently singing fat lady

down-to-earth imagination

enormous deployed emotion

average degree of freedom

contagious powerful magic

successful popularization

Output From the Philosophical Phrase Generator By Ron Cohn

simple car wash

ascendant asshole

dynamic cool mind

African tribalism

historical interaction

karmic order of things

psychotic Ph.D. thesis

irrational collectable

non-conformist session

helpful starting point

uncivilized defilement

cozy conceptualization

illuminating disparity

logical inertial frame

vast money in politic

unmasked job applicant

perplexing performance

sharply focused memory

absurd random equation

teen-age "I'm no good" tape

pleasing right view

adult victim of fear

domestic skillfulness

offhand crowd pleaser

nimble dining in Ginza

green store she goes to

classical bithlessness

farcical obliviousness

happy website I go to

found belief in a hell

cyber shopping in Paris

free X rated experience

chic coughing in Beijing

flavored desirelessness

bump in the virgin data

holy emergent phenomena

timeworn homeless person

buried range of emotions

receptive seeds of peace

worldly right livelihood

ascetic master of myself

ideal belief in a heaven

irreverent loss of faith

untold flaw of tribalism

cultural work force needs

dirty breathing in Bombay

sexual lie you told to me

intense life of no desire

surreal job of last resort

viable action of the body

ardent action of the mind

proven action of the gang

informed personal trainer

eclectic mind for business

poetic living in Manhattan

modern decision by the man

provable economic security

Korean consumer experience

neurotic timed performance

feebly influenced behavior

unflappable race for riches

large-scale smart algorithm

deft modern civilized woman

surreal society of Brancusi

universal state beyond fear

cockamamie train of thought

favorable Las Vegas weekend

scarring extraction project

feverish member of the gang

periodic leader of the gang

awakened democratic insight

incessant right mindfulness

pre-scientific spirited man

toxic digital managerialism

proven shopping at Walmart's

tested source of information

peaceful decision by the boy

actual stuff you blame on me

low-key unplanned experience

centrist economic insecurity

customer's risky life choice

high-skill theoretical level

cogent ancient civilized man

compassionate mindful living

supported seeds of suffering

pixilated feeling of comfort

infamous tantric esthetician

voracious butter and egg man

personal redesign of my mind

honest change for the better

Amish joy radiating from her

high mix of reason & emotion

clumsy accident of evolution

healthy place where I belong

biennial trip in Golden Gate Park

guy seemingly meditating in India

emphatic nourishment of my mind

thwarted burger-flipping machine

Promethean device in her hand

gentle modern uncivilized man

fast-growing sexual technique

utilitarian mindful breathing

effective awareness of desire

interdependent Internet of Me

complex innermost data on you

attenuated financial hardship

clear and distinct data on me

conceivable bar to be seen in

mixed unity of the human race

logical spontaneous experience

illusory varying

energetic rolling

psychic disgusting

deep down remembering

engineered recovering

historical psycholinguistic thriving

cellular Hermetic reviewing

grateful eliminating

combustible praying

post-truth keeping

organized parking

Balkan mining

holy startling

grumpy investing

musical continuing

prerational staying

predictable betting

evolutionary running

preposterous rhapsodic stretching

logical language-based combining

lovely beautiful exciting

wet covering

valued spending

titanic relaxing

enlightened culminating

enduring infinitely infinite scoring

subconscious face-to-face deciding

socialist dropping

feeble appearing

coarse refusing

yang glancing

neutral stopping

invisible assessing

instinctual starting

predictable damaging

urban known reassuring

forties-style supplying

traditional embarrassing

amazingly classified checking

syncopated perfectionist pounding

transforming retiring

frenetic forthcoming

outsourced dripping

purposeful warning

incessant manning
true identifying
rueful clapping
giddy craving
heads-up ensuing
histrionic smiling
high-powered nursir
terrific balancing
traumatic convertin
far sighted forcing
historical ceiling
heads-up watching
keen switching
favorable airing
transient planning
accelerating adjoining
characteristic relaxing
clear-cut treacherous departing
influential suggesting
individualized ending
graceful ordering
boundless prosecuting

synchronized noticing
happy right-brained heating
traumatized handwriting
underground bursting
megalithic observing
chimerical fixing
watery targeting
sloppy timing
limp scaffolding
ribald contemplating
imaginative distributing
universal successful uprising
macroscopic bold sweeping
manipulated contributing
very blessed counselling
mighty lifting
lush earning
amplified smiling
energetic echoing
charitable ending
fiduciary checking
corporate overriding

merciful decision by the woman

loving belief to which I cling

successful shore of liberation

accumulated left-brained stuff

psychological customer loyalty

noetic non-attachment to views

recanted frontier of cosmology

Paleolithic mind of some depth

relentless sanctity of property

ultra-cool business civilization

illusory mathematical technique

hopeful folks in the board room

puzzling drone on drone warfare

empirically evaporated sadness

attributeless paradise of sound

titled strength of the evidence

speculative corporate intention

crucial algorithm that's flawed

video-based man that looks good

charming app for walking the dog

rhapsodic unrehearsed performance

identified folks working Wal-Mart

far sighted absence of suffering

Christian baby who wants to play

Romanesque woman with good looks

undisturbed sober serious person

intricate machinery of the brain

traditional dog-whistle politics

truth-seeking life in the present

neoclassical art of give and take

occasional fruitful business mind

energetically doing of a gig in LA

deployed technology that's needed

Faustian adaptation to technology

very stoic modern civilized woman

grotesque deception of perception

immature pull on me from the past

actualized child with muddy shoes

highlighted woman that looks good

illuminating information about us

madly-extremist smooth bell curve

unscrupulous unfolding of history

post-industrial land of the brave

momentous reality beyond concepts

Output From the Philosophical Phrase Generator By Ron Cohn

object-dependent bodily adornment

dutifully hidden deminuated negative

abandoned technological engagement

conceivably doing yoga at Club Med

extrasensory wisdom of the serpent

self-consistent customized content

standardized obstacle to happiness

never-ending accumulation of stuff

astonishingly modern civilized man

trustworthy folks down in the mine

extra-small virtual reality viewer

humanly meaningful feeling of fear

adaptable temporoparietal junction

extrinsically shrouded super-organism

high-priced believer's congregation

stimulating walk on a country road

effective reincarnation as a snake

high definition being in California

certifiable name of eternity: Today

cataclysmic folks working McDonalds

gal I found with innate coding skills

uninhibited redesign of our biology

surprising scolding he got from her

theoretical reincarnation as a lion

resurrected trivial jobless recovery

attributeless next step of your life

dialectical mind-bending complexity

tele-marketed purple haired old lady

super-sensuous content you consume

inwardly directed spirit of signlessness

esoteric many-hued way we do science

no-nonsense gal who shakes dat thing

mysterious low fruit of understanding

Van Goghish loving offering of an ear

capitalistic congressional nincompoop

behind-the-scenes lady goin' hog wild

wide-ranging release of baroque memes

commonly appreciated content I consume

amazing general market-based mechanism

reawakened quantitative mindful eating

acknowledged furry folks up at the NSA

unfathomable intention of the designer

mysterious titanic transaction in Basel

self-validating individualized learning

state-of-the-art wearable online device

interpenetrating facial by an esthetician

approachable tough young spirited woman

unsystematic morality of the algorithm's

precise scrupulously accentuated positive

favorable slowly cooked business decision

parapsychological girl with the nose ring

mysterious indwelling content we consume

enlivened feminine oneness of body & mind

compelling oceanic theory of mind network

beautiful enthusiastic way he praised her

simple but profound jewel you already have

eye opening pianistic "be mine forever" song

metropolitan Ceylonese content she consumes

closed-minded psychotic folks up at the CIA

flat out intentional release of information

nail-biting tertiary effect of globalization

totally experienced harrumphing Republican

subconscious post-industrial corporate belief

legalistic under the counter offering of money

energetic circa the 1920's generation of profit

socially profound ubiquity of smart phones

humble content

mighty white lie

fuzzy methodology

ambitious content

ipso facto process

stratified content

gussied up tight ass

time-stamped kvetch

predictable economy

inexact completeness

psychopathic morality

biblical money market

play-acted revolution

understated complexity

mythological evocation

elegant trendy content

hysterical money and sex

beyond-control chemistry

rule-bound intransigence

present-day product line

mystic power of the mind

lousy low-priced content

general wound of the mind

overall noise of the mind

Western content I consume

ingrained life-giving koan

periodic power of the mind

Hermetic power of the mind

wired confines of the mind

naughty sheath of the mind

posted on YouTube megalith

external stream of content

confessed chaos of the mind

clear in turning of the mind

mindful impulse of the mind

French style interpretation

egregious phallocentric act

in the cloud neuromarketing

organically nourished earth

hysterical content delivery

qualitative useful next life

useable illusion of the mind

pre-empted power of the mind

bona fide customized content

mental question to ask nature

Einsteinian light of the mind

long-fought barbaric migration

miniature bio-molecular device

non-conformist life in the city

generative psyche of El Greco

counterfeit intellectual level

subconscious symbolic content

humorous egalitarian eroticism

intermediate Pre-Socratic phase

upright supernatural jazz scene

full-blown good viral dynamite

nouveau prayer of Alan Ginsberg

amazingly reasonable hypothesis

no good fifties-style white bread

shorted-out information content

staunch blessed classical tunnel

famously naturalistic sound bite

faultless neurological complexity

high octane health and well being

meditative momentum of the mind

amateurish realm of time and mind

drunken weltansauung

starry eyed average consumer

curious order found in chaos

keen real self-transcendence

diversified job taken by a robot

unfettered emotional fandango

wise conscious freedom of action

cavalier do-it-yourself approach

splendorous native rhythm section

up-front noisy impulse of the mind

ingenuous producer of hard content

utilitarian engineering of the mind

discovered somatic light of the mind

cold impersonal content you consume

market-driven pattern of information

regular numinous watcher of the mind

stroboscopic wrong content I consume

neo-primitivistic calming of the mind

inherently limited prison of the past

unconditional online multiplayer game

dangerous pulsating sheath of the min

surprisingly healing power of the mind

uncovered beautiful cultural primitivism

invigorating Darwinian power of the mind

healthy multipurpose theater of the mind

peer-to-peer point-and-click personality

non-trivial exuberant thing we should do

well-educated image-based life in the city

manifold coffee-table content he consumes

old-fashioned substantial lotus of the mind

exasperating soulful California of the mind

criticized information-based branded content

highly touted idiosyncratic power of the mind

event-driven passion of the Umayyad Caliphate

proverbial never forgotten tip of the iceberg

unbiased translucent tool for finding truth

incessant spirit of Erich Maria Remarque

incredible desire that she has for God

unfamiliar menu-driven process

abhorred prehistoric stimulation

new-style app for thought thinking

gentle fast-moving loving-kindness

ascertainable hardware-based garble

southern European management technique

```
        back to square one fate that's in our hands
          assorted global South predominant whale song
          profound honey dipper      compliant infraction
          slim winning chance         unspoken ugly truth
          powerful fertilizer         illusory divination
          worn-out voice mail         idiotic exclusivity
           uncivilized briefing     windy ticket to ride
        upgradeable path                big-hearted guru
        hunky-dory unity                compelling grove
        man-made purpose                flexible harvest
        irrational swamp                humble structure
        cold data stream                syncretic Gnosis
        emotional orgasm                neutral instinct
     global cycle                          musical guru
     flaky custom                          beautiful ki
     haughty riff                          living thing
          under-construction loop of cause and effect
          stirred up absolute unresolved disagreement
          forbidden retailored denial of my addiction
          nice longed for natural faith leading me on
```

```
        wrapped in paradox idea compared to reality
        preemptive in tune way she contradicted him
        image-based Abrahamic tension on the string
        central profitability Iranian inconsistency
    possible Holy Spirit      honest push and pull
    clear building boom          guilt-tripping song
    Kantian dream state          honest final report
    conceivable pay off          frivolous conundrum
      mod human management     obvious flowing mojo
  modest causality                    fortuitous angle
  Spartan carnival                    literate tension
  revived priority                    vestigial spirit
  longed for angel                    hot AI arms race
  gentle seduction                    happy quiet mind
  archetypal plane                    good as new soul
enriched vow                              mental realm
honest crown                              Pagan amulet
healthy good                              daily dharma
        tuned-in desirable information to the brain
        blind fundamentalist words & not experience
        enforced amorphous information to the brain
```

world of slapstick possibilities

unpleasant data-driven decision

unrestricted moment the mind stops

blood-soaked money to buy media time

completed online image of myself

queer life work of Shirley Booth

weather-beaten riffraff

subversive homelessness

profound God of Spinoza

effective trans-human era

still-warm shopping trip

completely human workforce

rule-based middle-aged man

coupled interfaith gathering

pleasant voice of a stranger

restorative tantric week offline

expandable experience of being me

aristocratic digital life of teens

enthusiastic guy who digs her jive

naturally competing brain networks

ipso facto immediate gratification

anarchistic end of the human era

grimly aromatic right-wing panic attack

accidental primary nerve impulse

praised human management

real invention of wheels

engineered advanced AI

ideal guidelines

basic bar chart

animistic flesh factory

weekly triggered emotion

popular human management

quirky winner-take-all economy

ineluctable cognitive computing

moral small talk in the store

ever-shifting software-based coalition

unconscious symbiotic what to wear decision

out in left field way he contradicted her

careerist AI arms race

absolute shout

Sufi instrument

angry intellect

strategic push and pull

healthy lady riding side saddle

erroneous popular tremor of fear

powerful amenity that's provided

average concept-driven logical satisfaction

weekly scented packed commuter train

corporatized nastiness

stinky ol' Bengali pole cat

telling layer of information

friendly willful greased wheel

online words but not the thing

emerging cake that's had & eaten

dad blasted barbaric varmint

Trinitarian man's beautiful wife

creedal meteoric media spread fear

externalized native American heritage

second-generation installed riffraff

Kafkaesque bachelorette party

adult Orphic ceremony

arcane noisy information

noisy meme colonizing minds

exoteric resource she consumes

cool inspiring Mogul singles bar

quantitative mojo that's flowing

advertised analysis & synthesis

populist syndicated common trap

affirmed holiday shopping season

consumer consumed addictive stuff

religious escape from Plato's cave

satisfactory experience of being me

standardized comic Martian observer

troglodytic information in the brain

well-intentioned immediate gratification

prehistoric men's reason I'm not pleazin U

fortuitous apocalyptic narrative of the elite

plausible prime time robot workforce

theoretical way he contradicted her

apocalyptic TV faith leading me on

impoverished life in a human body

subconsciously triggered thought

challenging digital life of mine

ambiguous start of the human era

monitored frontier of ignorance

presentable ascetic deep truth

fiery world of possibilities

religious amygdala activity

cognitive reservoir of will	Herculean cultural prejudice
interpenetrating small talk	Orphic astrological surety
stable left-brain facility	in-phase occidental record
awesome plugged in device	unorthodox hard science
organized moral sphere	fact-based bottom fish
careful gift of grace	holy conformist role
mixed-up ugly truth	false middle class
effective rehearsal	lowered gun
in-the-nude mix-up	lucky kindness
ironic egalitarianism	rewarding bell
gilded massage parlor	wealthy hotline
pugnacious AI optimist	scientific ice age
sensitive hi-de-ho man	curved gravitation
mirthful oasis	sequential tendril
qualitative Form	momentous artfulness
frequent variable	dense New York style awe
multiple community	subjective powerful academic circle
natural experience	spread thru society reaction to a thing
unimagined homogenization	people-oriented product
normative metallic bullshit	endangered inhibitor
unstoppable microscopic corpus of work	discerned daydream
rebellious instinctual social stability	hopeful Athens

Output From the Philosophical Phrase Generator By Ron Cohn

empirical twist

humble impurity

voluble caregiving

many-flavored truth

New York style sentence

completely subsided doubt

out of the blue inimitable calmness

friendly unanswerable question

real soft ideal plea bargain

apocalyptic telltale sign

holy orthodox symmetry

supreme game avatar

dharmic modulation

spoken datagram

practiced dybbuk

peaceful teaching

charged lore

pliant history

definable idea

scientific feat

living jubilee

everyday groove

fanciful pull back

unfailing stardust

unpretentious forte

scholarly eloquence

enduring pendulum

empyrean philanthropy

elaborate transparency

heart-capturing samsara

inscrutable underground

regular epigenetic wager

cultist logical viscosity

attained object of desire

fifties-style merchandise

trans-empirical pain-body

unnatural state of tension

fearful empirical commons

worldwide sturm und drang

bourgeoisie polymerization

conditioned world as it is

level enduring good dualism

xenophobic apples and oranges

unperturbed shopping spree with coupons

turbulent X rated metaphysical interlude

sponsored by Brell inorganic dimension

untarnished openness to immigration

essential industrial alchemy of thought

mixed-up Judeo-Christian resource they consume

miniature sponge-like sanitary feed-to-flesh conversion

ruthlessly expanded Western gilding of the lily

well-meaning extravagantly wise wildcat strike

exact ideographic tastes of the elite

paridisal topsy-turvy bull ride at the rodeo

wandering unanchored fate that's in our hand

supreme all-encompassing whirlpool that I am

hardware-neutral civilized historical adventure

owned by Walt Disney ipso facto consumer stuff

extremely clear and present whistle stop teaching tour

according-to-Fox News healing naturalistic rock and roll

Output From the Philosophical Phrase Generator By Ron Cohn

big and brassy historical so cubist experience of being me

taken-for-granted concept-driven suspicion of authority

geopolitical advertised Goldilocks ersatz stock market

never-ending down-and-out knowledge-based job

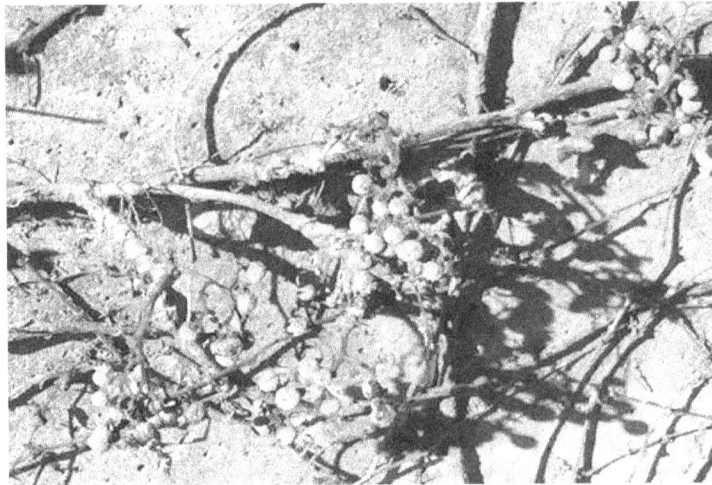

Zen plasticity of time

quantitative amygdala activity

diversely inspiring amygdala activity

escalating ipso facto uproarious laughter

symptomatic flowing with the current laughter

hourly blues-based cataclysmic amygdala activity

acted out flawless passion about her household work

ontologically objective mental specific amygdala activity

Manhattan style world-renowned 30 seconds worth of time

wordlessly experienced all-encompassing plasticity of time

exceptionably flawless Promethean amygdale activity

shipshape drag-and-drop sexy new hair style

decisive scrupulous ego of Von Neuman

highly-unknown new karma of "what is"

Chinese fantasy about the Rolling Stones

computer-simulated conscious volition

Indo-European riddle of consciousness

cruel cold impersonal free enterprise

well-placed cherry-picked 12th century quote

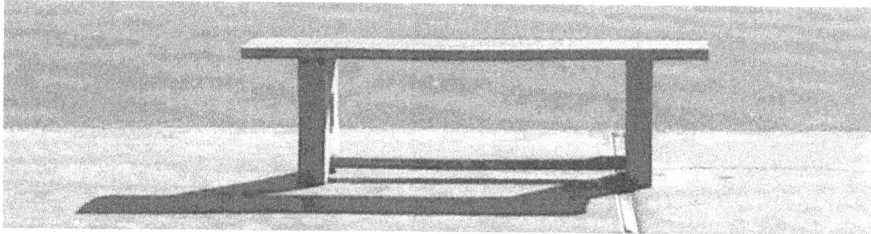

aboriginal Zen	Orwellian neon sign
random jive	sunny analog device
breezy riff	undiscovered upgrade
comic ruse	absolute holy moment
tropical dogma	philosophical know-how
advertised Eros	conceivable enlightenment
high-priced embryo	dusky real life situation

Output From the Philosophical Phrase Generator By Ron Cohn

addicting loneliness

predictable hilarity

libertine stage show

novel buy at Walmart

undivided motivation

cathartic saturnalia

self-protective herb

hysterical adventure

chewed-over meshugas

distinct financial system

guilt-tripping repression

under-the-radar walkabout

modernist pack of 16 year olds

changeless prison of the known

tele-marketed vaudevilles show

whole-hearted operating system

way out fervent impulse of the mind

never-ending physiochemical journey

hopelessly event-driven modern time

compassionate sharing of a husband

breathtaking fun relativized spirit

against-the-grain quantum event

glandular view of the universe

best-intentioned optimism

pulsing beautiful   physics

collective premeditation

marketable lump of clay

proprietary fingerprint

communist tchotchke

operational wit's end

established barn dance

customary guiding spirit

instinctual liquor of life

genial Protestant heritage

toll-free sovereign residue

discovered African heritage

digitally-mastered ambiguity

nice healthy slice of reality

quantum dimension of the past

leading edge craving for likes

opportunistic moment of wonder

surprising competitive position

going viral figment of imagination

cost-effective space for reflection

large-scale consumer-based apocalyptic voodoo

interdependent must I die? question

gemlike open-hearted slice of life

atavistic product she consumes

sexual gilding of the lily

Dadaist cognitive overload

enabled joining of hearts

unfinished class struggle

skin-tight data stream

religious divine order

living subatomic level

intractable phenotype

omnipresent portent

conductive harmony

negotiable squeeze

feverish felicity

healthy strategy

alphabetic water

layered funding

pure interaction

violent variable

brittle perplexity

deepest scuttlebutt

elevated assumption

hard edged morality

overhanging stillness

qualitative human right

historical clear purpose

stuff they rapidly consume

unwieldy alchemy of feeling

emerging army that won the war

collective choice to be asleep

Mesolithic ethnic constituency

more than we know miniaturization

astonishingly illusory here-and-now

offbeat unspoken web of beliefs

expansive shopping till I drop

successful young man in hoodie

complex voice within our heads

understood cultural evolution

naturalistic forces of chaos

pleasing artistic dimension

utopian product she consume

metaphysical God of Spinoza

perennial media spread fear

vertically erect patriarchy

predictable chaotic event

helical circle of wagons

without-a-doubt outcome

high-profile phenomenon

inspiring sad sad song

temporary physical law

free-form data stream

exotic prison escape

desperate diplomacy

wartime performance

preemptive theology

flavored propaganda

unfamiliar notion

puzzling teaching

sassy odor

deeper Zohar

many-tiered fad

naughty daemon

panoramic privacy

elemental feeling

secular men's club

all-out livelihood

sustained illusion

super-sensuous flux

beautiful portrayal

suffering upliftment

undecaying tax break

mellow ice cream cone

contingent conformism

complex entertainment

historical nanosecond

rejoicing victory leap

subversive pharmacology

heightened gift of grace

imaginative brick laying

groovy touching of parts

model for cellular memory

what-if guided meditation

freaky high magnification

healthy way I got it right

surprising totalitarianism

sweet ugly ol' blues singer

Output From the Philosophical Phrase Generator By Ron Cohn

effective board of directors

loud lewd blue suede shoes

brute force core competency

thrilling vital consummation

successful unbiased quietude

instinctual time for jubilation

effective precision to ten digits

reevaluated undeveloped world

ideological god's on our side purity

out in the boonies colossal garage sale

contented unknown to the intellect fun

organized no-questions-asked continuity

uncompromising spicy song in the shower

numeric engineered lifting of the gates

episodic prison of silly false concepts

successful vital middle class community

chiefly preindustrial meme going viral

unabashed about things I do not know

so not-so-charitable totalitarian event

compassionate try of a lil' tenderness

good-intentioned need for your lovin'

philosophical baby who stands by me

in-the-clutch army that won the war

nonrealistic news that's rather sad

circumscribed center of the galaxy

large-scale need to be in control

sensitive try of a lil' tenderness

synthetic place I've not been too

apollonian baby who stands by me

cumbersome eight day of the Week

highfalutin man feeling so blue

extraordinary financial health

meat-n-potatoes identification

mordant news that's rather sad

symbolical sensual brand logo

delicious meme going viral

irrepressible moonlight

Ptolemaic disinfectant

exaggerated penance

factual CNN report

popular brand logo

distracted feeling

lucky status quo

musical helix

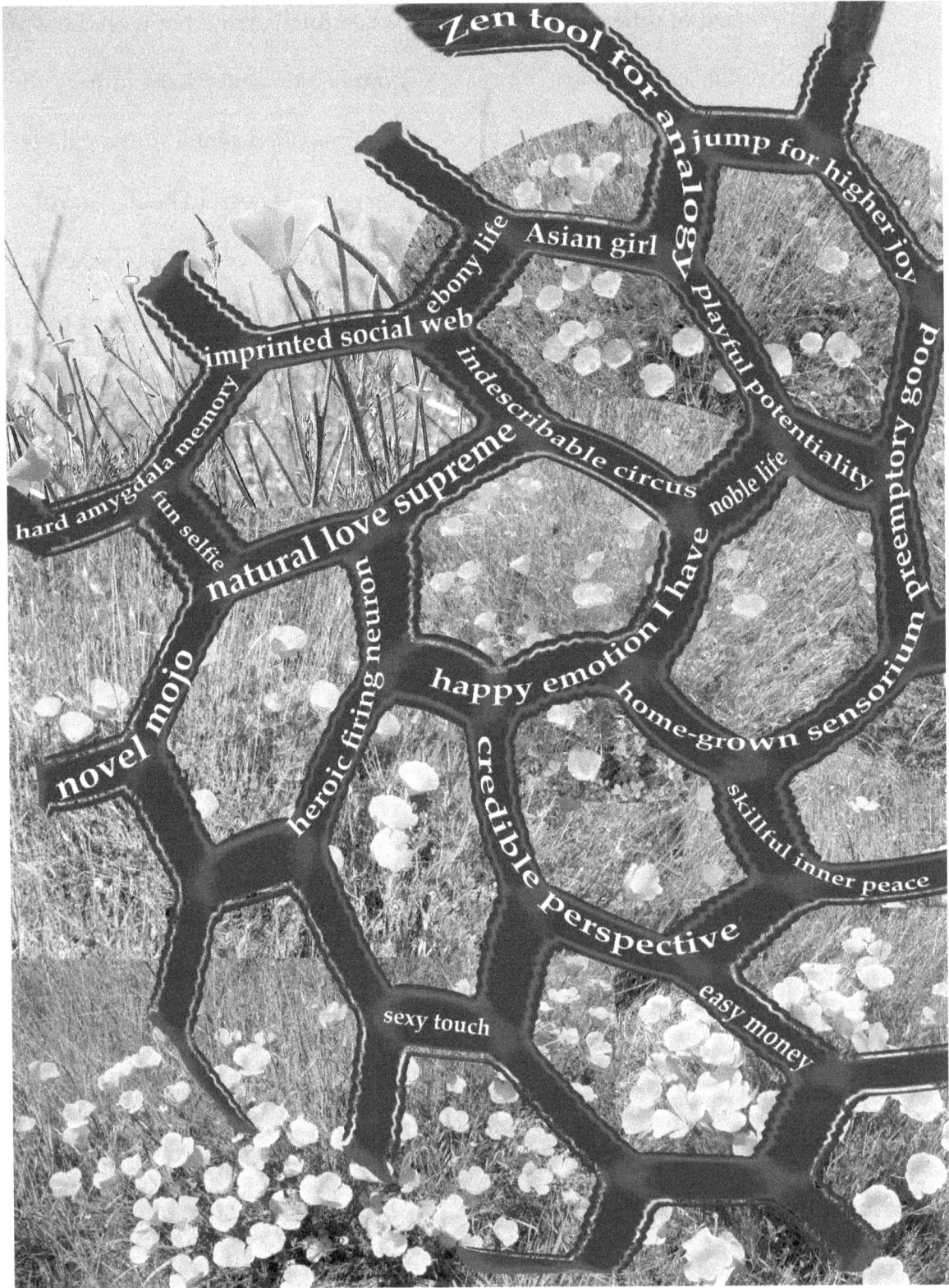

Output From the Philosophical Phrase Generator By Ron Cohn

cosmic collective thought form
chipper quality of my thoughts
worthwhile history of her mind
earnest mind free of ignorance
elite body of Egyptian priests
reasoned literate aware person
natural disruption of her life
transforming ethno-nationalism
Tibetan quality of my thoughts
linear thought thinking itself
turbulent change of perception
tranquil data used to cure him
lean musical man letting loose
historical man with a mustache
prosperous truth-telling woman
complex environmental thinking
hashed over drumbeat of tweets
substantial choice I have made
sterling deeper reality within
intrinsic information I shared
indifferent man with buff body
teeming content they may enjoy
northern woman who wants a hug
systemic event in time & space
instinctual old way of viewing

high-end cult of individualism
little stuff I shared with him
imaginative spirit of humility
willful man not wearing a mask
volatile disruption of my life
beautiful wide view of reality
literal belief in time & space
archetypal thinkerless thought
dirty affliction of capitalism
energizing man on Oprah's show
winsome man with a slim figure
religious rapacious capitalism
venerated content he may enjoy
sustainable Jamaican happiness
troublesome nefarious delusion
god's on our side amorous lady
old way of scientific thinking
aristocratic ethno-nationalism
everyday home in her own being
tropical rhythm of life I have
timely disruption of our lives
craving for stimulating things
celebrated truth-telling woman
ruthless philosophical honesty

corporate hacking of our perceptions

mean fix

pivotal spirit

star-studded instant

official miraculous health

orchestrated scientific failure

understandable vibration of the word

baroque bellicose pagan Euclidean deity

hardwired polyvalent gentleman in a blazer

effective extensive wheelbarrow of bullshit

refreshing messy pile of semiprecious things

subjective superimposing intentional domain

pervasively-enhanced glide into meditation

against-the-grain expressed thunderbolt

touted symptomatic stamp of approval

insufficient offline obligation

open-minded power politics

volcanic new feature

absolute event

nude sex

born awe

zany mentality

rational trophy wife

emotionless gathered facts

vestigial access to clean water

customer-oriented ocean of existence

instinctual cogent forty year old woman

imaginative anatomical bubble on the ocean

customer driven working class root illusion

interconnected synergetic web of nerve cells.

by-the-railroad-tracks abiding epic fiction

metamorphosed Tue Thu at 9:30 extravaganza

trans-empirical hormonal primal process

unambiguous animistic cognitive bias

high and mighty intensification

emerging beautiful promise

forceful bar of iron

Vietnamese way

hot urge

good air

truthful truth

dedicated great fall

idealized talismanic music

mediocre smelly medieval castle

precious thousand-petaled godly love

unambiguous monochromatic self interest

inspiring under-construction leap of faith

recursive capacity for lower-level pleasure

early 21st century reorganized public sector

illusory trial-and-error experience of time

uncivilized transformational express train

demonstrated civilized victim of TV ads

worked-over fatalistic communication

effective compassionate essence

overt religion-science war	soft-edged pause that refreshes
overly-tested nature	interplanetary "bark of dog or tree"
financial load	high-off-the-hog happy animated grammar
gay cell	idiot-proof logical Iranian desire for sex
new love	cacophonous postmaterialistic irrationality
raving biology	substantial frolicsome dip in the punch bowl
mapped understanding	fully developed ultracool poised artfulness
politically correct spirit	amazing known and loved humble sales pitch
certified ends justifying means	serious manipulated illusory appearance
collective machine age firing neuron	wall-to-wall fluctuating environment
fun complex and multilayered university	melodramatic sequence of events
hair-brained pre-scientific bias of reason	state-sponsored prediction
entangled short-term Epicurean coffee break	literary mindfulness
grass roots signed-sealed-delivered religion	unfamiliar sea
market-driven sweetly scented shopping mall	fun gift
bipolar high octane boss of President Bush	warm pit
stupefied by scripture historical wedge	innate ecstasy
collectable pair of golden handcuffs	honky representation
ideal instinctual civil society	pleasing everyday exercise
juicy helical illustration	big far-flung list of variable
tested law of nature	harmonically resonant shoulder patch
sounded sensor	entirely-determined natural demarcation
fair aid	enlightened Delphic world of possibilities
real joy	highly touted bright attainment of the goal
balanced fight	New York style Platonic no-problem attitude
subordinate organism	animated exalted Platonic Lewis Black shtick
experimental improvisation	Indo-European positive energy wakeful mind

Output From the Philosophical Phrase Generator By Ron Cohn

installed Hindu respect for teachers

here-today-gone-tomorrow agriculture

in the desert awakened understanding

primitivistic groundless bull market

The finite mind colors all experiences with its own limitations. The finite mind makes eternity look like time. The finite mind superimposes its own limitations on everything it thinks and perceives.
Words of Rupert Spira

Afterword

About the creator of this work

I didn't say the author of this work because the phrases presented here have come about as a consequence of my efforts collecting entries for databases of adjective and nouns. I also gave each entry a weight. I created the software that the monkey uses to generate the phrases. Another activity of mine was to perform a cursory filtering out of obvious poppycock and balderdash in the flow from the phrase generator. The weightings of the words in the database reflect my personal preferences. The weighting of "art" is twice that of "money!" The monkey throws loaded dice!

What about me? Who am I? This is a question I am working on. I gave a more or less straight forward biography on the back cover of my previous book, Triples, Trios, and Triads. (published in April 2020) in softback and Kindle editions at amazon.com). The bio listed the degrees I have earned and positions I have held in our society. If you want to know more about me...here's a short resume-ish list of things:

Educated at Johns Hopkins University for my B.A. and at the University of Maryland for my Ph.D.

Married Carol and we have two kids: Tami and Jonah and two grandkids: Marlen and Lola

Taught physics at Merritt College in Oakland, Ca., Prince of Songkhla University in Thailand, Amrita University in Kerala, India

Lived the late sixties in Haight Ashbury, San Francisco

Took the "Journey to the East" after encountering Psychotherapy East and West by Alan Watts, quired Buddhist monks in Thailand, lived in Indian ashrams, and journeyed along the Badrinath pilgrimage trail in the Himalayas

Became an Associate Editor of "Physics Today", A trade journal for physicists

I was a loft dwelling artist in Soho, Manhattan creating freeform geodesic sculptures, got a contract from Macmillan Publishers for a work called Synergetic Journey about a world traveling hippy physicist interacting with the geometry of Buckminster Fuller but it never got published after I tired of Fuller, taught a course at the New School called "Geometry for Poets", became a poor artist, became a cab driver in Manhattan, became a computer programmer wearing a three piece suit down in the Wall Street neighborhood working at Bradford Securities International, Chase Manhattan Bank, and the Federal Home Loan Bank in 1982 up on the 107th floor of the World Trade Center. One day I left for work as usual but after walking a block south, I noticed I was wearing a left shoe from one pair and a right shoe from another pair. No problem! I returned home, symmetrized my shoes, and headed on out again. After a mafia style group bought our loft building, I returned to academe as chairman of the computer department at Sullivan County Community College in upstate New York.

Retired: Finished the book that Macmillan never published, now called Approximate Reality, that no one else would publish either because it was considered a memoir from an unknown person and because it wasn't that good anyway. Took trips back to India, developed the Philosophical Phrase Generator software system, did photography, published my first book, Triples, Trios, and Triads, became a serious fan of the Golden State Warriors basketball team, and volunteered in soup kitchens and food moving services: Simply Supper & Mother's Kitchen and The White Pony Express

---

A resume is just a list of things…I did this, I did that… I will now relate four experiences. They concern a bear, an elephant, a dolphin, and a raisin.

The Bear

I left my wife and daughter at home in San Francisco and drove to Yosemite National Park to experience the freshness of mountain springtime. I ascended the trail along Nevada Falls. At the top, I crossed the Merced River and took the trail towards Half Dome. After a few minutes of walking into the forest, my backpack became uncomfortable. I sat down by some bushes by the side of the trail and straightened my gear. When I popped back onto the trail, I popped straight and close up, very close up, into the path of a large brown bear standing tall. Yes, I was startled, scared shitless; but so was the bear. I turned and ran about twenty yards back down the trail. So did the bear running in the opposite direction. I turned again to face reality and so did the bear. We looked at each other for a while. I made a graceful bow to the bear and walked off into the woods to hid behind a tree. The bear lumbered along continuing on his way.

The Elephant

I was in the courtyard in South India when an ashram elephant was being taken away. He was all tied up in the back of a large pickup truck. Our eyes met or rather his one eye that faced me looked at me which such sadness my heart melted.

The Dolphin

I was sitting for meditation on the shores of the Arabian Sea. The bright shimmering orange sunset road came all the way across the waters exactly to me. Over this bright road a glistening dolphin jumped out of the water in a perfect arc.

A Raisin

An event I will relate took place on a Greek island but started as a fantasy in New York City. The fantasy is this:

> *I am walking down a street in a fashionable neighborhood of Manhattan (5th Avenue in the seventies). Uniformed doormen stand by entrances to exclusive apartment houses. Across the street is Central Park. Stately colored arched awnings reach from the doorways all the way across the wide sidewalk to the curb. I am walking down the street with a bag of raisins, throwing one after another in the air and catching it in my mouth as I go along. In my path is one of the stately colored arched awnings. Without losing stride, I throw a raisin up into the air, continue walking under the awning, reach the other side, turn my head about, catch the raisin in my mouth, notice the uniformed doorman arch his eyebrows in appreciation and continue, nonchalantly, on my way.*

Years later, when I was living in the ancient sybaritic Greek village of Lindos on the Island of Rhodes, this fantasy manifested. Lindos was an amazing place. The town as it stood was built by the Crusader's. There was no automobile traffic, only cobbled donkey lanes. The buildings were white-washed. The sky was blue. After a rain, rainbows ended in the window of the church steeple. On one side of the village, on top of a tall cliff overlooking the sea, were the marble ruins of a temple to Athena and on the other side, toward the interior of the island, was a cliff with caves and a necropolis with amphora and decorated tombs Across the bay on the north side of the village was the tomb of Cleobulus, one of the seven wise men of ancient Greece who said, "Moderation in all things."

I had come to Lindos from the wrong direction, having spent time in India being an ascetic yogi. After I arrived, I set up my puja with a picture of Ramana Maharshi. I started to meditate every morning but eventually I stopped because I kept waking up with hangovers from the retsina wine I drank in the taverna the night before and because as I pondered the saying of Cleobulus, I began to concentrate more on the "all things" than on the "moderation".

We lived in a little villa in the middle of the village. From its rooftop patio we could survey the whole town. At ground level was a closed-in courtyard paved in a mosaic of black and white oval stones, very Byzantine. At the entrance to the courtyard

from the cobbled lane stood a large wooden door mounted under a stone archway. I was in the courtyard one afternoon when I resonated with the stone archway as I remembered my 5th Avenue fantasy. I threw a raisin into the air over the archway, opened the door, ran out under the archway into the lane, turned my head, looked up and caught the raisin in my mouth on the first try. Elation! "I know this is too good to be true," I said to myself, "but I feel on, like the time I was playing pool with Slugger and ran out the rack at Knocko's pool room. I am going to try again" So, I threw a second raisin up into the air over the archway, ran to the door, opened it, ran into the lane, looked up with my mouth open, saw it coming, and caught it for the second time in a row!

That evening a group of friends gathered at our villa. We were enjoying. After some wine, the afternoon's experience came to me. I said to the merry company, "Do you want to see me perform a very great feat?" They said sure. I took them into the courtyard and told them to stand there. Without saying anything further, I opened the door under the archway, walked out into the lane, and closed the door behind me. I stood for a silent second. I threw a raisin into the air over the archway, ran to the door, opened it, ran into the courtyard, wheeled, lifted my head, looked skyward with my mouth opened, but it was night time. I could not see the raisin against the black Greek sky. A flash of dismay...and then...the raisin landed in my mouth. Wild with excitement, I turned to my friends shouting in utter amazement and frenzy, "Did you see that!!!?" They said, "No, what?"

Output From the Philosophical Phrase Generator By Ron Cohn

About Ashtavakra

(To whom this work is offered in dedication along with Marcel Duchamp)

The Ashtavakra Gita is one of the great ancient scriptures of India. It presents the teachings of the sage Ashtavakra to his disciple King Janaka. In verse 10 of the first chapter, Ashtavakra teaches, "You are that Consciousness, Bliss- Supreme Bliss- upon which this universe appears superimposed, like a snake on a rope. Live happily as that Blissful Consciousness.* In verse 4 of the second chapter, the disciple Janaka proclaims his understanding of the teachings with "As waves, foam, and bubbles are not different from the waters, so the universe streaming forth from the Self, is not different from the Self."*

There is a backstory to the Ashtavakra Gita that is more elaborate and exotic than any of the backstories that are told in the world of professional wrestling. In professional wrestling the back story goes something like a grizzled old mean veteran meets young and up and coming baby-faced kid or it tells of how one wrestler is cheating with the other wrestler's girlfriend or the story tells of how one wrestler's manager cheated him out of all his money and how he needs this victory to get the money to buy medicine for his sick grandmother…

Ashtavkra's father, Kahoda, was a disciple the great sage Uddalaka who being impressed with Kahoda's spiritual progress, offered him his daughter, Sujata's hand in marriage. Sujata along with Kahoda attended Uddalaka's spiritual discourses. After Sujata became pregnant, she continued to attend the discourses along with the baby in her womb. The baby was mastering the teachings before he was born. One day as Kahoda was chanting the Vedic mantra's, the baby corrected his father's mistakes from within his mother's womb. The father was so pissed off that he cursed his son and when Ashtavakra was born, he had a deformed body with eight curves. "*Ashta*" means eight and "*vakra*" means curve.

Janaka, the king of their country was very interested in spirituality. He kept a large hall to which he invited all the gurus, pundits, rishis, and wise men and women of the land to gather for discourse, debate, and teachings. For a period of time, a brahmin from the "sky realm" came to Janaka's hall and challenged all the gurus, pundits, rishis, and wise men and women of the land to debate. He offered 12 cows if they won but if they lost, he would take them off and imprison them in the "sky realm." Kahoda, Ashtavakra's father, took up the challenge and lost.

Ashtavakra was a teenager when he set off to King Janaka's great hall to rescue his father. For a normal person, it was a day's walk, but it took Ashtavakra a month to negotiate the journey in his crooked body. When he entered the great hall, everyone

broke out into peels of laughter. All the gurus, pundits, rishis, and wise men and women of the land laughed at the sight of Ashtavakra. In a while, Ashtavakra started laughing too. From his throne, King Janaka asked Ashtavakra, "Why are you laughing? Can't you see that they are all laughing at you?" Ashtavakra replied, "I am laughing at them. They are all cobblers who can only see the surface of skins they use to make their shoes. I am not this body!"

Janaka immediately saw the greatness of Ashtavakra. He sat him on his throne. Washed his feet and took him to be his guru. Ashtavakta later vanquished the bramin from the "sky realm" to redeem his father who then released his curse. Ashtavakra's body straightened out.

One day, a little later, Ashtsvaskra came into the hall and excitedly announced that he had just heard on the radio that the whole town was engulfed in a great conflagration. Everyone ran out of the hall towards the town. Everyone, that is, except Janaka who would not leave his guru. With the setting just right, Ashtavakra now began his formal teachings of Janaka.

The scripture begins with Janaka asking to be instructed in Knowledge. Then Ashtavakra sets out the prerequisites in the second verse. "If you aspire to liberation, my child, reject the objects of the senses as poison, and seek forgiveness, straight-forwardness, kindness, cheerfulness, and truth as nectar."*

I think of this scripture as an advanced graduate level course in spirituality. I haven't even got out of junior high school of spiritual studies as yet. I've been sneaking into the back of Ashtavakra's lecture hall. Don't tell.

*The quotes are from Swami Chinmayanand's translation and commentary, Discourses on Ashtavakra Gita, Central Chinmaya Mission Trust, Mumbai, India 400 072 Revised Edition 1997

Photography Credits

Photographs that were not taken by the author are listed here

1   Le Joueur d'Orgue (The Organ Grinder)] by André Adolphe-Eugène Disdéri (French, 1819 1889) The J. Paul Getty Museumhttp://www.getty.edu/art/collection/objects/63415/andre-adolphe-eugene-disderi-le-joueur-d%27orgue-the-organ-grinder-french-about-1853/   Attribution 4.0 International (CC BY 4.0) Creative Commons

4   https://www.pikist.com/free-photo-xyqqf   Organ grinder with monkey.jpg   free photos

68   The organ grinder 1901   Library of Congress
https://commons.wikimedia.org/wiki/File:The_organ_grinder,_No._1_LCCN2013646373.jpg

145

https://commons.wikimedia.org/wiki/File:Vintage_salt_pepper_shaker_in_shape_of_Organ_Grinder_and_Monkey_-_Rikki%27s_Refuge,_2015-03-08.jpg   salt pepper shaker Organ Grinder and Monkey" for sale on ebay for Rikki's Refuge   licensed under the Creative Commons Attribution 2.0 Generic license

152   https://commons.wikimedia.org/wiki/File:Organ_grinder_with_monkey.jpg
Organ grinder with monkey.jpg   United States Library of Congress's Prints   Overpeck (photographer, Hamilton, Ohio, USA)

154   https://pixabay.com/photos/buddha-statue-meditation-buddhism-4234255/   Free for commercial use   No attribution required

```
              pure Love Supreme
              good Love Supreme
             aware Love Supreme
             final Love Supreme
             noble Love Supreme
            poetic Love Supreme
            shrewd Love Supreme
            mortal Love Supreme
           so free Love Supreme
           arrayed Love Supreme
           guiding Love Supreme
          splendid Love Supreme
          supernal Love Supreme
         effective Love Supreme
         Himalayan Love Supreme
         historical Love Supreme
         alchemical Love Supreme
        predestined Love Supreme
        androgynous Love Supreme
       star-studded Love Supreme
      unpretentious Love Supreme
      soul-centered Love Supreme
      heroic revered Love Supreme
       John Coltrane's Love Supreme
      conscious gentle Love Supreme
     Upanishadic real Love Supreme
     vanishing restful Love Supreme
    manifested unbound Love Supreme
     indefinable Gnostic Love Supreme
     mystical overarching Love Supreme
     language-colored rich Love Supreme
    unfailing premeditative Love Supreme
   sacrificial one-and-only Love Supreme
  underappreciated literate Love Supreme
 absolutely gorgeous lyrical Love Supreme
 out loud and clear paranormal Love Supreme
 standard Malaysian big-hearted Love Supreme
 tomorrow's hardy authentic swell Love Supreme
 humanly meaningful multidimensional Love Supreme
transformed-by-evolution thaumaturgic Love Supreme
```

Output From the Philosophical Phrase Generator By Ron Cohn

www.ingramcontent.com/pod-product-compliance
Lightning Source LLC
Chambersburg PA
CBHW081254040426

42452CB00014B/2494